The Shorter MBA

Barrie Pearson, BSc, FCMA, is Executive Chairman of Livingstone Guarantee plc, specialists in acquisitions, management buy-outs and corporate finance. They are advisers to companies ranging from household name multinationals to unquoted companies. Pearson is the author of *Realising the Value of a Business*, *Common Sense Time Management*, *Common Sense Business Strategy*, *Successfully Acquiring Unquoted Companies*, *Manage Your Own Business*, *How to Buy and Sell a Business* and *The Profit-Driven Manager*.

Neil Thomas, MA (Cantab), is Managing Director of Hawksmere plc, seminar and training specialists. He was the originator of the highly successful *Developing the High Performance Manager* course.

Mark Thomas is a director of Performance Dynamics, a consultancy specializing in organization change and transformation. He was formerly with Price Waterhouse Management Consultancy and has also worked with the NCR Corporation and Unigate.

Barry Turner, BSc, MSc, CEng, FIMechE, FRAeS, MILE, MIProdE, FBIM, is an independent consultant with an extensive background in engineering, project management, lecturing and writing.

D1422026

The Shorter MBA

A Practical Approach to Business Skills

Contributing Editors

Barrie Pearson
Neil Thomas

Contributors

Neill Ross
Mark Thomas
Barry Turner

HarperCollinsBusiness

HarperCollins*Publishers*
77–85 Fulham Palace Road,
Hammersmith, London W6 8JB

Published by HarperCollins*Publishers* 1997
1 3 5 7 9 8 6 4 2

First published in Great Britain by
Thorsons, an imprint of HarperCollins*Publishers*, 1991

ISBN 0 00 255830 0

Typeset by Harper Phototypesetters Ltd.
Northampton, England

Printed and bound
by Scotprint Ltd, Musselburgh

Contents

Introduction and Acknowledgements

About the book

This is designed to be a practical book to cover the key aspects that you need to address in order to be commercially successful in business. It is divided into three main parts:

- Personal development
- Management skills
- Business development

The structure and format of the book will enable you to grasp the essential ingredients of:

- Personal success . . . of high achieve-
ment, time management, personal effectiveness, solving problems/ decision making and effective communication skills;
- Management success . . . through understanding finance, project management, human resource management and competitive marketing strategy;
- Business success . . . through strategies for growth, preparing a business plan and through the buying and selling of unquoted companies.

The concentration throughout is on tips and techniques to give a practical approach to effective business skills for personal and business success.

Barrie Pearson,   Neil Thomas
Livingstone Guarantee plc

About the authors and contributors

Contributing editors

Barrie Pearson BSc, FCMA is the Executive Chairman of Livingstone Guarantee plc, acquisitions, disposals, management buy-outs and corporate finance specialists. They are advisers to companies ranging from household name multinationals to unquoted companies. Barrie is author of eight best-selling books in the area of finance and management, including *Realising the Value of a Business* and *The Profit Driven Manager*, and his approach to strategy is featured in two video films, *Business Strategy* and *Time Management*, both produced and distributed by Hawksmere.

Neil Thomas MA is Managing Director of Hawksmere plc, seminar and training specialists, and was responsible for the original concept and development of Developing the High Performance Manager (The 5 Day MBA!) course which has proved so popular and successful. He also has a wealth of publishing experience which he has brought to bear in pulling the varied contributions in this title together in a cohesive manner.

Contributors

Competitive marketing strategy
Neill Ross MA is a Consultant specializing in Marketing and in Property Management. In preparing the section on Marketing, Neill Ross and the Contributing Editors gratefully acknowledge being able to draw on notes taken during presentations by Braxton Associates.

Human resources management
Mark Thomas BSc(Econ), Dip PM, MIPM is a director of Performance Dynamics, a consultancy specializing in organization change and transformation. He is experienced in the development of Human Resources Strategy and Organization Development programmes in both the private and public sectors. Formerly with Price Waterhouse Management Consultants, his previous personnel operations experience includes the NCR Corporation and Unigate Group.

Project management
Barry Turner BSc, MSc, CEng, FIMechE, FRAeS, MICE, MIProdE, FBIM is an independent consultant. He held the first Chair of Industrial Management at the University of Newcastle on Tyne, was Adviser and Technical Administrator with GEC/EE Company and is a former Principal of the English Electric Staff Training Centre at Dunchurch. Prior to this he was Assistant Director of Engineering with English Electric after being Chief Projects Engineer with the British Aircraft Corporation. He has published many papers on training and project management and is the author of several books.

Part 1
Personal
Development

High Achievement

1.1 Analysing yourself

The essential ingredients for success are to:

- decide what personal success you want
- create a personal vision of success
- adopt a quantum leap approach
- believe success will happen
- focus on success goals
- be undeterred by set-backs.

The starting point for high achievement in your personal and business life is to review positively your strengths and weaknesses. A basic self-assessment should review:

- What am I good at?
- What do I enjoy doing or would enjoy given the chance?
- What kinds of business would I like to work in or to own?
- What are my assets?
- What work situations, frustrations and stresses do I wish to avoid?

Questions such as these should be asked of ourselves at regular intervals to provide opportunities to focus on what we would like to make happen and to aim for the high achievement of desired results.

1.2 Setting goals

High achievement depends on first of all identifying and setting goals, then setting about making them happen by addressing and dealing with those key issues on which success or failure depend.

Three-year goals

- The goal(s) I will achieve within three years are: _____
  _____
  _____
  _____

- Sub-goal(s) which need to be achieved are: _____
  _____
  _____

One-year goals

- The goal(s) I will achieve within one year are: _____
  _____
  _____
  _____

- Sub-goal(s) which need to be achieved are: _____
  _____
  _____
  _____

In setting these goals you should adopt a quantum leap approach to achieve dramatic results, e.g. to triple profits within three years.

You must fix on these goals and use iron determination to make them happen by focusing on the reasons for achieving success:

- My success goals are important to me because: _____
_____
_____
_____

- My success goals are achievable because: _____
_____
_____

_____
_____

- The obstacles to be overcome are:___
_____
_____
_____
_____

- The priorities to focus on are:_____
_____
_____
_____

CHAPTER 2

Time Management

2.1 Assessing your time-management skills

Time management is not an end in itself. It is the means to an end. It has to be linked with setting and meeting goals and, in this way, it provides the way to leverage really high achievement out of the individual and others with whom they come into contact.

How do you rate your time management skills? Do you:

(1) Have success goals written down? YES/NO

(2) Agree your success goals with your boss wherever he/she should be involved? YES/NO

(3) Give the impression to people that you are well organized, really on top of your job, and still have time for people? YES/NO

(4) Find enough time to tackle the important projects? YES/NO

(5) Have a reputation for invariably meeting deadlines? YES/NO

(6) Ask your secretary which jobs she/he could do for you? YES/NO

(7) Work away from the office occasionally to concentrate on a particular job? YES/NO

(8) Reply to correspondence quickly? YES/NO

(9) Regularly return telephone calls sufficiently promptly? YES/NO

(10) Do you make enough use of technology and office equipment to save you time? YES/NO

(11) Deliberately decide to leave certain jobs undone, until someone complains? YES/NO

(12) Make a list of what jobs and telephone calls must or should be done today? YES/NO

(13) Often take work home or go into the office at weekends? YES/NO

(14) Feel it is better to do a job yourself than to train someone else to do it for you? YES/NO

(15) Allow people to waste your time by dropping in for a chat? YES/NO

(16) Do you literally open the post each morning? YES/NO

(17) Write things in longhand for your secretary to type? YES/NO

(18) Spend time doing jobs which a junior person could do as well as you? YES/NO

(19) Arrange your own meetings? YES/NO

(20) Waste time filing things or finding files and information? YES/NO

(21) Sometimes go home feeling the day has been consumed by interruptions? YES/NO

(22) Accept telephone calls YES/NO

during informal meetings?

(23) Spend too much time in unproductive meetings? YES/NO

(24) Arrive late for meetings quite often? YES/NO

(25) Spend too much time being chased by others and chasing others about missed deadlines? YES/NO

(26) Are you too much of a perfectionist for your YES/NO

own good?

(27) Accept requests to do something, when it makes more sense for someone else to do it? YES/NO

To be rated a 100 per cent effective manager, you should have answered YES to questions 1 to 12 and NO to questions 13 to 27. How did you perform? Is there room for improvement?

2.2   Focusing on results/opportunities

In order to use time management techniques, it is vital to be results-driven and to do this effectively means identifying key results and assessing major opportunities as follows:

Key results to be achieved in order of importance (time spent on them, ranked 1 to 5):

(1) _____
_____ deadline: _____

(2) _____
_____ deadline: _____

(3) _____
_____ deadline: _____

(4) _____
_____ deadline: _____

(5) _____
_____ deadline: _____

The major opportunities to be pursued in order of importance (time spent on them, ranked 1 to 5):

(1) _____
_____ deadline: _____

(2) _____
_____ deadline: _____

(3) _____
_____ deadline: _____

(4) _____
_____ deadline: _____

(5) _____
_____ deadline: _____

2.3   Using your diary for better time management

The trick is to plan *your year first* and *your day last*.

(1) Enter key year planning dates in your diary:
● regular meetings for the year

- known one-off events (e.g. AGM, Sales Conference, trade fairs, budget preparation)
- holidays
- family occasions
- key tasks (e.g. strategic workshop, Far East visit, customer visits).

(2) Plan your next month and:
- count unplanned days available
- duck less important events
- reserve a meeting-free day each week
- reserve key task time.

(3) Plan this week
- develop regular habits (e.g. weekly team lunch, Friday p.m. in the office).

(4) Plan each day at the outset and:
- develop regular habits
- fix management-by-walking-about (MBWA) or open door times
- set personal assistant (PA) times
- list and rank jobs and phone calls
- use PA to follow up
- make daily action lists
- remember 'stress' can be reduced by planning to use your time to tackle areas of concern

How to manage each day

- Plan each day at the start or better still the night before.
- Make a list of tasks, work out time needed for each and prioritize.
- Isolate the key task and make sure it gets done.
- Don't be too ambitious and clutter each day with tasks that can wait.
- Build a time for solitude and/or to handle an issue that could crop up.
- Reduce interruptions from phone calls, visitors, etc. at times ear-marked for task completion.
- Tie each day in with the week, the month, the year and your goals.

(5) Follow up effectively by using three follow-up files:
- this week
- next week
- this month.

(6) Diary/daily planning format
Adopt a system which can accommodate detailed timings and sections (in each day) to list 'tasks to be done' and 'phone calls to be made'.

CHAPTER 3

Personal Effectiveness

This chapter summarizes a variety of areas that should be addressed in seeking ways of improving the way you operate in business.

3.1 Appearances

You should make your own and your office appearance reflect *now* the achievement of your success goals. An action plan is needed for:

● your own appearance – hair, weight, clothes, etc.
● your office appearance – walls, ceilings, tidiness, decoration.

Create a successful achieving style and remember *you never get a second chance to make a first impression*.

Perhaps the most important aspect of appearance (and one which affects the ability to tackle important tasks) is how your desk is managed.

Ways to clear your desk

● Don't leave any papers on it when you leave.
● Don't have papers out for more than one task at a time.
● Don't keep papers hanging around:
  – diarise when to action and then file them,
  – dump unwanted items,
  – pass on with action notes (hand-written, don't wait for typing up).
● Don't let filing pile up (do it yourself if need be).
● Don't get side-tracked reading items that should be put in a separate to-be-read file or pile.

3.2 Handling your manager

It is vital to agree with your own manager (or fellow directors) what will constitute high achievement in your present job.

A key results statement needs to be agreed and listed in order of importance:

(1) Key result: _____

Standard of performance: _____

Priority/deadline: _____

(2) Key result: _____

Standard of performance: _____

Priority/deadline: _____

(3) Key result: _____

Standard of performance: _____

Priority/deadline: _____

In arriving at this agreed list, you will need to:

● understand the constraints and pressures on your manager
● receive an appraisal of your performance
● negotiate the resource and the support needed to ensure success

● obtain the support needed for high
achievement.

You should list the external and internal
obstacles to be overcome:

(1) Obstacle: _____

　　Action needed: _____

　　Assistance requested from: _____

(2) Obstacle: _____

　　Action needed: _____

　　Assistance requested from: _____

(3) Obstacle: _____

　　Action needed: _____

　　Assistance requested from: _____

You should agree the major opportunities
to pursue and win positive help and
commitment to them. A check-list would
be:

(1) Purpose and results to be achieved:
_____
_____
_____
_____

(2) Proposal: _____
_____
_____
_____

(3) Other tangible benefits to be
produced: _____
_____
_____
_____

(4) Methods to be adopted: _____
_____
_____
_____

(5) Costs and timescale required: ____
_____
_____
_____

(6) Financial return to be achieved: ___
_____
_____
_____
_____

3.3 Delegation and team-building

It is essential to lead by personal example
by:

● defining your goals in writing and
believing you will achieve them
● identifying key results
● using your appearance and style to
reflect achievement of your success
goals
● planning to overcome internal and
external obstacles.

You will need to recruit people who will achieve outstanding results and to create and maintain an atmosphere of excitement in which high achievement will flourish. You should ask people whether they:

- want to achieve the key results
- believe they can be achieved

and ask them what will:

- make their jobs more interesting and enjoyable
- have to be done in order to ensure results are achieved

and what can they contribute by way of:

- ideas to overcome difficulties
- ideas for new opportunities to be pursued.

You need to select what to delegate by identifying key tasks and for each one note down:

- which member of your team could do this job
- what exactly is stopping you giving the task away
- what you will do to give the task away effectively.

You should then make lists of:

- tasks to be given away to other team members; and
- extra time which you can then invest on key tasks of your own.

Formats for these lists might be as follows:

Tasks to be given away to other team members:

	time to be saved
(1) Task: _____	
_____	
To be given to: _____	
Action needed: _____	
_____	
Target date: _____	
_____	

time to be saved

(2) Task: _____

To be given to: _____

Action needed: _____

Target date: _____

(3) Task: _____

To be given to: _____

Action needed: _____

Target date: _____

Extra time to be spent on key tasks:

time to be invested

(1) Task: _____

Action to be taken: _____

Target date: _____

time to be invested

(2) Task: _____

Action to be taken: _____

Target date: _____

(3) Task: _____

Action to be taken: _____

Target date: _____

In order to delegate effectively (once you have identified the time-consuming tasks to delegate and identified key tasks to spend more time on) you need to:

- agree the results and the standards to be achieved
- agree the deadlines and the completion dates
- agree any interim check-points
- explain the importance, the context and the constraints
- provide the authority needed
- police the agreed deadlines rigorously
- say thank you when deadlines are met
  - literally
  - write a note
  - with flowers or wine.

You must invest time now to develop your team and should discuss with each person:

- their success goals
- training and development needed
- job satisfaction
- their next job or project.

In respect of training and development programmes, each person should have one and a sensible format is:

Name: _____ Year: _____

Training to be completed: _____

_____

_____

_____

_____

Personal development to be completed:

_____

_____

_____

_____

Delegation check-list

- Don't let subordinates 'delegate' to you.
- Don't delegate only the work and not the authority.
- Don't delegate and interfere (other than at agreed check-points).
- Don't delegate and forget to follow up.
- Don't delegate without agreeing objectives/results expected.
- Don't delegate and let the problems come back rather than the solutions.
- Don't delegate and delay matters by withholding decisions/information.
- Don't delegate without discussing workloads.
- Don't withhold praise.
- Don't do a task if you delegate it.
- Don't confuse delegation with abdication.

Finally, in *recruitment*, you should remember:

- to replace people incapable of outstanding achievement
- you have the team you deserve
- to pay well for outstanding achievement
- recruit resultaholics not workaholics.

To *create an atmosphere of excitement* to breed high achievement you must:

- exude enthusiasm – it is contagious
- *sell* not *tell* key results
- discuss how to make work more enjoyable
  - invite ideas
  - consider prizes/competitions
  - visits to trade shows, branches, etc.
  - sponsored events
- keep people informed of results.

If you aim to *reward high achievers* (e.g. they should be promoted unselfishly because that policy is one of enlightened self-interest) you should also decide to tell people (in private) immediately when their performance falls short, otherwise you are condoning mediocrity.

In summary, the best ways to *create a winning team* (and create 'free time' for yourself) involve:

- leading by example
- recruiting people for outstanding achievement
- injecting excitement
- giving freedom by delegation
- investing in staff development
- promoting outside your team.

As a brief introduction to the more formal ways of team operation, a structural and results analysis of some different ways of working in teams can be summarized as follows:

Type of team	Structure and function	Results
Problem-solving team, e.g.:	• 5-12 volunteers/ employees from different 'areas' of a business or department	• can reduce costs and influence quality • do not result in changes in work efficiency or involve managers enough

Type of team	Structure and function	Results
	• meet 1-2 hours per week • discuss ways to improve quality, efficiency, etc. • no power to implement ideas	• fade away over a short period
Special-purpose team e.g.:	• design and introduce work reforms and new technology • link all separate functions • involve management, unions, etc. • make operational decisions	• creates high level involvement • can make wide changes
Self-managing team, e.g.:	• 5-15 employees who produce entire product • members learn all tasks and rotate jobs • handle all managerial duties	• can increase productivity very significantly (research shows by 30 per cent) • fundamentally change an organization • employees more in control of their jobs • eliminates supervisor level

3.4 Meetings

Formal meetings

You should first of all test how effective your current formal meetings are by using this check-list:

(1) Was the action agreed worth the time spent in preparation, attendance and minute writing?

(2) Was the total amount of time spent by those attending justified by the action agreed?

(3) Why should the meetings continue to be held?

(4) Why do you need to attend the meetings? Why not delegate the job to someone else and attend only when the situation or agenda merits your contribution?

(5) Why not hold them quarterly instead of monthly, or monthly instead of weekly, or only when either actual results to date or year-end forecast is more than 5 per cent below budget?

(6) Who needs to attend regularly? Who

should be invited to attend when relevant? Who only needs to receive the minutes for information?

(7) Do you compile or authorize the agenda?

(8) Are the agenda and background papers circulated soon enough for people to come adequately prepared?

(9) Do the meetings start on time with everyone present?

(10) Do you check at the start of the meeting that the actions arising have been completed?

(11) How long do the meetings last? How long should they be allowed to last?

(12) Do you manage to complete the agenda within the scheduled time regularly?

(13) Do people know when the meetings are scheduled to finish? Do they finish on time?

(14) Is personal accountability and a deadline assigned to each action item?

(15) Why are the minutes not restricted to a list of actions agreed?

(16) How soon after the meeting are the minutes circulated? Why aren't they circulated within 24 hours?

(17) How long do you spend either writing the minutes or approving them?

(18) What percentage of items are actioned by the due date?

(19) Why do you tolerate less than virtually 100 per cent?

(20) Have you asked those attending the above questions?

You can make your formal meetings more effective by focusing on:

● *Timing*
  – treat starting time as sacrosanct
  – schedule to finish at lunchtime/end of day (any overshoot would be unwelcome by all)
  – only give time to the key issues.
● *Agenda*
  – write it yourself
  – make it specific
  – put important items first
  – circulate in advance (and insist people prepare).
● *Minutes*
  – reduce to action, person responsible and deadline summaries
  – circulate within 24 hours of meeting.

Informal meetings

You should first of all test how effective your current informal meetings are by using this check-list:

(1) Do you always telephone to find out when it will be convenient for the other person to meet?

(2) When you telephone, do you briefly mention your purpose and agenda so that he/she will be prepared? And indicate how long a discussion is needed? And ask if there is anything else he/she wishes to discuss to ensure you are prepared?

(3) Whenever you meet with your manager, if you have a problem, do you always outline the answer you recommend and are able to mention the alternatives you have rejected, and your reasons, if asked?

(4) Do you hold regular informal meetings with your staff to avoid frequent and unnecessary interruptions?

(5) Do you insist that they must never bring a problem to you without hav-

ing considered the available options and recommending a solution?

(6) Do you waste people's time by answering the telephone during informal meetings?

(7) Do you ask members of your team to come to your office without the courtesy of telling them your agenda?

(8) How often do you visit members of your team rather than have them always visit you?

(9) Whenever someone telephones you to suggest a meeting, do you always ask the purpose and the priority needed?

(10) Whenever someone visits your office for an informal meeting, do you suggest another time if you are not sufficiently prepared or it will interrupt a key task?

(11) Do your meetings always end with decisions approved or specific action and a deadline for completion agreed?

Effective informal meetings usually have this profile:

● telephone in advance to agree
  – purpose
  – agenda
  – convenient time
● attendees should bring problems and answers
● telephone interruptions should be avoided
● decisions should be made with action and deadlines agreed.

Some tips for successfully handling informal meetings include:

● MBWA (management by walking around):
  – you visit your staff (they don't interrupt you)
  – you see for yourself
  – you maintain contact.
● visit people in their offices to meet, rather than letting them visit you, because then you can decide when to leave.
● stand up – sitting can prolong an 'informal' meeting.

3.5 The telephone

You must be ruthless in ensuring that you master the best ways of using the telephone to your advantage to ensure that you are using your time effectively and getting results.

Your policy must be to only take calls when and from whom you want. Effective time managers invariably have a policy of not taking incoming calls but operating a call back system (i.e. making the calls when they want and when they are prepared to do so).

Key tips are not to receive calls when:

● interviewing
● in an informal meeting
● with a client or a supplier
● in a formal meeting
● you don't want a key task or your creativity to be interrupted.

It is usually better to group calls for a particular time in the day and you should think in advance what you wish each call to achieve. You should reduce time wasted on finding numbers, dialling numbers and making social calls by using your PA to best advantage to get the people you want (and give a list of people, not one at a time) and to keep a good system of regularly updated numbers and best contact times.

You should use your PA to screen callers (and ask 'why?') and to handle routine calls or re-route them. If you are out or don't wish to take a call, the PA should take a message and find out when to call back.

Time wasters should be handled by telling them you only have a few minutes (and they should be called at lunchtime or after hours when they are less likely to take up your working time).

3.6   Personal productivity

The following is a summary of key ways in which you can boost your own productivity:

In-tray action

- have PA stop unwanted mail
- scrap junk mail
- stop unwanted magazines
- re-route items before they reach you
- remove yourself from unwanted internal circulation lists
- get PA to sort mail into:
  - urgent action
  - team mail
  - reply or action
  - information only
- batch-process correspondence
- scan and dump the unimportant
- separate 'to action' items
- put to one side 'to be read . . . some time' items
- aim to handle items only once.

Read effectively

- preview long reports by reading the summary, the conclusion/recommendation and scanning the charts/graphs
- read with your eyes – don't subvocalize – and scan and skip
- cope with figures by
  - reading headings
  - the horizontal lines
  - look at key figures
  - ignore uncontentious detail
  - check footnotes
  - ask for exception summary or get PA to highlight.

Reduce filing

- use waste-paper basket
- file address/phone number only
- use central filing for company/team
- put correspondence in date order
- separate bulky reports
- use dividers
- purge and archive
- *or dump.*

Travel productively

- commute off-peak if possible

- use time to read and plan your diary
- minimize travel to meetings by having people come to your premises.

Benefit from information technology by finding out about

- personal computers
- desk-top publishing
- on-line information services
- teleconferencing
- electronic mailboxes
- remote banking services.

3.7 Personal motivation

It is crucial that you master ways to motivate yourself as it is self-evident that without it, you will not only fail to achieve your goals but also you will fail at motivating others to help you to achieve them.

What follows then is a self-motivation check-list (to be used whenever you feel your motivation is flagging).

Self-motivation check-list

- Focus on your goals and keep difficulties in perspective.
- See your problems as opportunities.
- Become a resultaholic not a workaholic.
- Set deadlines.
- Work on the important not the seemingly urgent.
- Take time out to think.
- Develop non-work interests and activities.
- Write down your fears/problems/ frustrations and ways of overcoming them.
- Don't pass over a difficult task – start the day with it, or fix a time to do it.

The whole area of self-motivation requires separate study, but if a real motivation crisis is unfolding for you you should refer back to the section on High Achievement to try to focus on what you want to achieve.

Remember, too, that current research shows that the left side of your brain can be in 'conflict' with the right. You should be aiming to address certain self-motivation difficulties by using each part of the brain to compensate for the difficulties caused by the other.

Here is a comparison of the characteristics of the left and right sides of the brain:

'LEFT' BRAIN (dominant side)

- controls right side of body
- verbal
- rational, controlled
- logical
- reading, writing
- naming
- mathematical/scientific

'RIGHT' BRAIN

- controls left side of body
- non-verbal
- non-rational, emotional
- intuitive, creative

- face recognition
- artistic, musical, songs, understands humour

A useful technique to 'change your way of thinking' about a situation, particularly when you feel demotivated is to change a negative thought pattern into a positive one.

Negative approach

- I can't
- I should
- I hope
- It's not my fault
- It's a problem

- It's difficult
- If only
- It's terrible
- What can I do?

Positive approach

- I won't
- I could
- I know
- I am responsible
- It's an opportunity
- It's a challenge
- Next time, I will
- It's a learning experience
- I know I can cope

3.8 Business knowledge

High achieving managers need to ensure that they develop an effective knowledge of their business and the environment it operates in. To have an improving approach you should:

- read the trade press regularly
- scan the technical page of relevant newspapers to look for developments which may affect your business
- maintain links with relevant university research departments or industry research associations
- make sure you have the opportunity to meet major customers even if you are no longer directly involved in sales

- visit the point of sale for your products occasionally, e.g. the wholesaler, retail outlet, or your own branch, to know what is happening
- meet with existing and potential suppliers occasionally to find out about their developments
- visit the major exhibitions in your industry sector to keep informed about competitors
- visit other countries expressly to meet overseas competitors, or to find new sources of supply, or to assess export opportunities, or to find out what is happening there at first hand
- listen to your sales people to keep informed about your competitors
- ask your customers about the opportunities and pressures facing them so that you can respond to their needs.

3.9 The effective manager

As a reminder to yourself, you should keep in mind these 10 qualities which research has generated as being the hallmarks of the effective manager:

(1) Provide clear direction.
(2) Use two-way communication.
(3) Demonstrate high integrity.
(4) Choose the right people.
(5) Coach and support people.
(6) Give objective recognition.
(7) Establish ongoing controls.
(8) Understand financial implications of decisions.
(9) Encourage new ideas and innovation.
(10) Give clear decisions when needed.

CHAPTER 4

Solving Problems/ Decision-making

4.1 Effective decision-making

To be an effective decision-maker:

- you should identify the decisions which if made:
  - will have the biggest impact on the key results
  - will achieve a quantum leap improvement in excess of the key results which have been set.
- when making a decision, you should ask:
  - what result will be achieved?
  - what is the fundamental purpose?
  - what other options/opportunities should be exposed?
- you should consider the issues and identify:
  - what could go wrong
  - the obstacles you may face
  - any likely hostile response by competitors, trades unions, staff, etc.
- you should challenge the status quo:
  - why do it?
  - why not do it?
  - why this often?
  - why this standard?
  - why this way?
  - why here?
  - why this price/cost?
- you should always make decisions in time for them to be effective.

4.2 Solving problems

- The problems faced in solving problems can include:
- too much information
      spending time fact-finding
      not identifying key data required
- not planning ahead
      last minute realization of time difficulties
      not having adequate data
- not recognizing useful ideas
      doubting your own
      ignoring others.
- Successful approaches to problem solving lie in part in correcting the above 'problems' by
- clearly identifying the problem
  - writing it down
  - establishing the facts and objectives
  - considering a wide range of solutions
  - calmly reviewing options and ideas
  - focusing on results and desired outcome and not preventing solutions from presenting themselves
  - objectively choosing the best solution.
- Brain storming:
  - individual brain storming
      write down the problem
      write down at least 20 ideas and their opposites
      use lateral thinking (seemingly unrelated ideas)
      prioritize
      choose the best ideas
  - group brain storming
      appoint 'recorder'
      identify problem clearly in writing

allow free-flow (no criticism as you go) of ideas

select ideas to pursue
arrange follow-up action meeting

4.3   Handling crises

You should have your own personal approach to crisis management, to deal with crises as they will arise in business.

A helpful check-list is provided below for you to refer to at such times, but you should first of all test out whether you are good or bad at avoiding crises.

How to avoid a crisis:

- have a plan to handle potential crises (e.g. computer failure, post strikes, employee strikes, fire etc)
- anticipate change (do not merely respond when it happens)
- do not delay making decisions hoping a problem will go away
- do not respond to minor difficulties as if they were all major crises
- remember that if a crisis happens you should respond calmly but urgently.

How to handle a crisis:

- individually or collectively agree its identity and seriousness – define the problem
- state desired result
- list solutions
- test feasibility of preferred solutions
- choose and implement action plan without delay.

CHAPTER 5

Effective Communication Skills

5.1 Effective writing

- avoid writing whenever possible
  - don't merely confirm or acknowledge
  - telephone rather than write
  - use an internal memo and write your reply on it
  - produce standard paragraphs for PA to use
  - your PA should write routine letters
  - don't write to team members, tell them
- Write clearly
  - use a heading
  - use short sentences
  - itemize individual points
  - use short paragraphs
  - don't be frightened of using one-sentence letters

- be informal
- Effective reports
  - start with executive summary
  - summarize recommendation
  - outline financial justification and benefit
  - use precise key points and figures only
  - must be capable of making sense on its own
  - write on one side of paper only
  - bind them
  - have a contents page
  - number the pages
  - use dividers
  - relegate the back-up information to appendices
  - avoid 90° turns
- Business plans
  - see Chapters 10 and 11 on strategy and on business plans

5.2 Effective presentations

There are four essential steps to take to ensure that presentations in different situations are going to be successful. They are: preparation, gaining and keeping attention, maintaining interest and closing positively.

1. Effective preparation

- Informal presentation/meetings
  - define the desired outcome (check out support of key team members, if appropriate)
  - set the agenda (circulate if appropriate)
  - gather the data
  - spell out the benefits
  - summarize financial justification.
- Formal presentations
  - check out the venue and set up (numbers attending, lay-out, equipment available, etc.)
  - check time available for your presentation and how you will be introduced
  - check out who will attend and get background on them
  - rehearse your presentation (and check on slides, etc.)
  - expect to be nervous (but know that

'nerves' will fade after five minutes)
- try to meet attendees before your 'session' so that you will 'know' them.

2. Gaining and keeping attention

- Informal presentations/meetings
  - fix the best (most convenient/ distraction free) place
  - only start when you have the complete attention of the others
  - agree start and finish times
  - ensure there are no interruptions
- Formal presentations
  - make sure the audience is ready and seated before you start
  - deliver your opening sentence positively to command attention.

3. Maintaining interest

- Informal presentations/meetings
  - don't waffle; stick to the point
  - involve other people
  - focus on 'good news' and benefits
  - mention key opportunities/results/ issues in a way that will command attention
  - convince by showing financial justification, how it will work in practice and what the evidence is that it will work
  - talk with conviction.
- Formal presentations
  - tell people why the subject is important to them
  - tell them the topics you will cover (and when you would like to take questions – throughout or at end)
  - advise them of the decision/approval you expect, if appropriate
  - use flip-charts/slides/videos to hold

audience concentration
- use key words on slides
- don't read your presentation
- demonstrate your own conviction and enthusiasm in words, voice and gesture
- spell out benefits
- present factual evidence (not opinions)
- demonstrate financial justification
- show that potential problems have been identified and overcome
- handle questions as arranged and authoritatively.

4. Closing positively

- Informal presentations/meetings
  - close with agreement to the outcome you want
  - agree who will do what by when
  - if no agreement, try to ensure that some positive action is taken towards your goal.
- Formal presentations
  - ask for the approval, order or action you want to conclude your presentation.

General advice on presentations

- Rehearse, rehearse, rehearse.
- Use slides or flip-charts if possible
  - help structure presentation
  - allow audience to focus on key points
  - lets you look at audience while elaborating on the key points
  - keep information on each slide to a minimum (20 words or fewer figures)
  - make sure type on slides is big enough to be seen clearly
  - show slides in correct order (and

number them)
- use visual stimulus, e.g. cartoons.
- Work on your presentational style
  - entertain your audience with anecdotes, illustrations, examples
  - vary your voice (tone and level)
  - use 'jokes' sparingly if at all
  - avoid bad language, risqué jokes, etc.
  - avoid excessive walking about or extravagant gestures
  - involve your audience – let them question you, but also question them – don't hold on to fixed ideas, listen
  - let them hear, see and do: lecture, visual aids, worked examples/syndicate discussions, etc.
  - don't apologize
  - relax.

Part 2
Management
Skills

Finance

This chapter concentrates on the practical finance and accounting techniques needed to manage for profit and to generate the maximum cash flow from a business. It is divided into two main parts to provide the elements required in sound commercial practice on a day-to-day basis:

(1)   Technical aspects which need to be understood.
(2)   Techniques which can be applied.

6.1 Understanding the essentials

1. The Profit and Loss Account

There are usually presentational differences between 'internal' profit and loss accounts (prepared for internal use within a company, usually monthly) and 'external' profit and loss accounts (which are published annually) and are required to show more than merely the profit and loss for the financial year.

Basically, the profit and loss account is a statement of the income receivable during a given period, and the costs incurred in generating that income. The difference is the profit or loss. (It is the income receivable and not necessarily received in cash during the period. Similarly, it is costs incurred but not necessarily paid during the period.)

An 'internal' profit and loss account will tend to focus on:

	£
Turnover	X
less	
Direct costs	Y
Gross profit	Z
less	
Depreciation	
Provisions	N
Overheads	
Net profit	0

For 'internal' purposes the detail and the format will vary from business to business, but from a management point of view what matters is that a profit and loss account should give an accurate picture and one that enables the various component elements to be tracked accurately, so that appropriate decisions can be taken, on action that can be directly related to each element making up the profit and loss account.

The 'external' profit and loss account shows more than merely the profit or loss for the financial year. It also reveals:

● turnover
● some information on costs
● bank interest, payable and receivable
● taxation payable
● dividends to shareholders
● profit retained in the business to finance expansion.

In essence, the profit or loss is calculated by:

● the sales turnover or fee income invoiced, but not necessarily paid by customers, during the year

less the total of

● the costs incurred to produce the invoiced sales turnover or fee income, but not necessarily paid during the year

and

● the depreciation charged on assets owned within the business during the year.

Depreciation is the charge made to the profit and loss account, and the similar reduction in the asset value shown in the balance sheet, to reflect the value of an asset used up. Depreciation is frequently calculated on a 'straight-line basis'. The cost, less any estimated realizable value on disposal, is divided by the estimated number of years of the useful life of the asset. See pp. 54-5 for more details.

It is almost certain that the profit made by a business and the amount of cash generated will be different, because the profit and loss account is not based upon cash received and paid out during the financial year. Indeed, a profitable manufacturing company may consume cash during a period of expansion, because additional finance may be needed for:

- increased stocks of raw materials and finished goods
- the increased level of work-in-progress in the factory
- a larger amount of money owed by customers, which is described as debtors
- investment in capital equipment.

It would be understandable to assume that there is a standardized format for all profit and loss accounts, but it would be wrong. The presentation is broadly similar, but it is important not to be confused by different presentations.

Perhaps the simplest form of published profit and loss account is as shown below:

For the year ending 31 December 199-

	199- £m	199- £m
Turnover	603	570
Operating costs	540	515
Operating profit	63	55
Net interest payable	(9)	(12)
Profit on ordinary activities before taxation	54	43
Taxation on profit on ordinary activities	14	12
Profit attributable to ordinary shareholders	40	31
Dividends	13	10
Retained profit transferred to reserves	27	21

The published profit and loss account and the balance sheet need to be read in conjunction with the accounting policies and the notes to the accounts that accompany them in the Annual Report (see below) of each company.

The **Annual Report** contains the:

- chairman's statement
- report of the directors on the business
- statement of accounting policies
- audited profit and loss account, balance sheet, and source and application of funds statement
- notes to the accounts, providing supplementary information
- in the case of stock-market-listed companies, often includes historical performance figures over the past five or ten years.

The accounting policies explain the basis on which the accounts have been prepared, for example the method used to value stocks and work in progress.

The notes to the accounts provide the detail behind some of the figures shown in the profit and loss account and balance sheet, together with other supplementary information, e.g. details of directors' remuneration.

Typical descriptions of the terms used in the profit and loss account shown above are:

(1) *Turnover*: sales invoiced to customers during the financial year, excluding value-added tax (VAT). Only sales to third parties are taken into account for the profit and loss account of a group.

(2) *Operating costs*: consist of several items such as:
- cost of goods and services invoiced
- distribution costs
- research and development
- administrative and other expenses
- employees' profit-sharing bonus.

(3) *Operating profit*: is the profit on the normal trading activities of the company, before taking into account bank interest and taxation.

(4) *Net interest payable*: the net amount of interest receivable and payable on all overdrafts, loans, etc.

(5) *Profit on ordinary activities before taxation*: the 'profit before tax', but the use of the word ordinary is deliberate because there may be extraordinary items as well, which will be explained later.

(6) *Taxation on profit on ordinary activities*: is based on the profit for the year and takes into account deferred taxation which arises from timing differences between the taxation rules and accounting policies used by the company. These timing differences are commonplace, e.g. between capital allowances for taxation and depreciation, but disappear eventually. So deferred tax is provided for in the accounts only if it is expected to be payable.

(7) *Profit attributable to ordinary shareholders*: profit earned for the ordinary shareholders, after charging the liability for taxation arising on the profits.

(8) *Dividends*: the total cost of the dividend paid to ordinary shareholders.

(9) *Retained profit transferred to reserves*: profit after tax left in the business to provide additional finance for future growth and development.

Published profit and loss accounts often seem more complicated in real life. The only difference, however, is that other situations have arisen which need to be explained. They are really no more difficult to understand. Other terms which might arise include:

(10) *Other operating income*: examples

might be government grants, royalties and other income.

(11) *Share of profits less losses of related companies*: this applies to a group of companies and are companies in which the group owns between 20 and 50 per cent of the shares, and exercises significant influence on commercial and financial policy decisions. The share of profits consists of:
- dividend income
- share of undistributed profits less losses
- gains on disposal of investments
- amounts written off investments.

(12) *Attributable to minorities*: the share of profits on ordinary activities after taxation to which minority shareholders in subsidiary companies are entitled.

A subsidiary company is a company between 50 and 100 per cent of which is owned by a holding company, which means that effective management control is exercised.

---

(13) *Extraordinary items*: are events or transactions outside the ordinary activities of the business which are both material and not expected to reoccur frequently or regularly.

(14) *Reorganization costs; profit on sale of property*: can be shown separately below the line of trading profit, because although these are items which occur in the normal course of business, their size makes them significant and exceptional.

(15) *Preference dividend*: is the dividend payable on preference shares, which are usually entitled to receive the same amount of dividend each year.

(16) *Extraordinary items*: represents the net gain arising from the disposal and discontinuance of certain businesses.

Depreciation

Depreciation is charged on tangible fixed assets, excluding land, and intangible assets (see below) owned by a company. It is included as part of the operating costs. The most commonly used method to calculate depreciation is to write off the cost of the asset evenly over its estimated useful life, taking into account any residual value likely to be realized on disposal, where appropriate.

Intangible assets are items capitalised on the balance sheet by some companies, in addition to tangible fixed assets such as land and buildings, equipment and motor vehicles. Examples of intangible assets are goodwill, purchased brand names, research and development, and intellectual property purchased such as patents.

The estimated useful life of assets may be considerably less than the period for which they are physically usable. This applies particularly to electronic equipment. For example, a computer could still be usable after 20 years, but the company may choose a useful life of only five years for purposes of calculating depreciation on the assumption that by then it will wish to buy a more technologically advanced machine.

Depreciation does not necessarily adjust the recorded value of the asset to reflect the market or realizable value. An obvious example is the purchase of a motor car, because immediately the vehicle is driven away from the showroom the value of the tax charged on a new car has been lost. Another example is a piece of custom-built electronic equipment designed to test a particular product. The realizable value would be only the scrap value of the individual parts, assuming that it could not be used or adapted by another company.

It must be realized that the provision of depreciation as part of operating cost does not involve setting cash aside to replace the asset in due course. It is simply 'book-keeping entries' in the financial records of the company.

Companies usually define a specific useful life to be assumed for depreciating different types of fixed assets. Typically these are:

- freehold buildings – 25 to 50 years
- plant and equipment – 5 to 20 years
- motor vehicles – 3 to 6 years.

Consider the annual depreciation charge on computer equipment which cost £140,000 where the company assumes a useful life of five years and no residual value to be realized on disposal. The annual depreciation charge will be one-fifth of the purchase price, i.e. £140,000 divided by 5, which is £28,000 a year.

Internal Profit and loss accounts

Other terms which may occur in profit and loss accounts prepared for internal use within a company include:

- cost of sales
- gross profit
- bad debt provision.

Cost of sales

The cost of sales is more accurately described as the cost of goods and services invoiced. It is calculated as:

	£m
Value of stock and work-in-progress at beginning of financial year	430
plus	
Goods purchased and production costs incurred	2,248
less	
Value of stock and work-in-progress at end of financial year	(514)
equals	
Cost of sales	2,164

Gross Profit

The gross profit is calculated as:

	£m
Sales turnover	3,372
less	
Cost of sales	(2,164)
equals	
Gross profit	1,208

The selling and distribution costs, administration expenses and other operating costs are deducted from gross profit to calculate the operating profit.

Bad debt Provision

If a customer has gone into receivership or liquidation, and there is no chance of receiving even part payment of an outstanding debt, then the debt must be written off and charged to the profit and loss account.

At the end of each financial year, an estimate must be made of the eventual cost of likely bad debts as well as those actually written off. Accountants refer to these estimated amounts as provisions.

The charge to the profit and loss account each year is calculated by:

	£'000
Bad debt provision at end of year	52
plus	
Bad debt written off	17
less	69
Bad debt provision at start of year	45
Charged to profit and loss account	24

This may seem thoroughly confusing, but it is not. Bad debts of £17,000 have occurred during the financial year. In addition, the estimated amount or provision for likely bad debts has been increased by £7,000 from £45,000 to £52,000. So the total charge to the profit and loss account is £17,000 plus £7,000, namely the £24,000.

Dividend payment

Dividends of stock-market-listed companies are usually paid twice a year. An interim dividend is paid after the half-year results are announced. The directors recommend a final dividend, which is paid to shareholders after they give their approval at the annual general meeting. Many private companies either choose not to pay a dividend at all, or alternatively are likely to pay only a final dividend.

If the dividend is, say, 1.0p per share, then income tax is deducted at the standard rate. When this rate is 25 per cent, the shareholder receives:

● a net dividend payment of 0.75p per share

and

● a tax credit (see below) of 0.25p per share.

On the quarter dates, 31 March, etc. and the company's year end, following the payment of any net dividend to shareholders, the company is required to pay to the Inland Revenue the value of the tax credits as a payment of advanced corporation tax. This can be reclaimed by the company setting it off against future corporation tax payments.

> **Tax credit** When a dividend is paid to a shareholder, an amount equal to the standard rate of income tax is deducted as a tax credit in the UK. This means that the standard rate of income tax is automatically deducted in the same way as applies to building-society interest.

The actual amount of income tax payable by the shareholder on the dividend is adjusted annually by the Inland Revenue, for those who either are liable for the higher rate of income tax or are not liable to pay any income tax at all because of their low income. This is done as a result of the shareholder being required to declare net dividends and tax credits on his or her personal income tax return form.

2. The Balance Sheet

The balance sheet of a company published in the Annual Report provides a financial picture of the company at the end of the financial year, showing in essence:

● the assets and liabilities of the company

and

● the sources and amounts of finance used.

('Internal' and 'external' balance sheets tend not to differ very much, except additional detail may be presented internally.)

It should be realized, however, that the balance sheet at the end of a financial year may give a quite different picture compared to one prepared at other times. For example, consider a manufacturing company supplying gift items, with peak sales at Easter and Christmas. Stock levels are likely to be at their lowest in, say, February and October when goods have been shipped to wholesalers and retailers in readiness for the selling season. The overdraft is likely to be lowest in, say, April and December when customers have paid for their orders received in time for the peak sales periods.

Many business executives find the balance sheet much harder to understand than the profit and loss account. Some give up the attempt, assuming that the balance sheet is of little importance. This is a completely false attitude. Assets must be managed as aggressively as profits, and the starting point for asset management is a thorough understanding of balance sheets.

It would be convenient if one could safely assume that every balance sheet has an identical format, but the reality is that balance sheet formats are merely similar.

A simple balance sheet may have the format shown below:

Balance sheet at 30 June 199-

		199- £m		199- £m
Fixed Assets		407		351
Current assets	177		167	
Creditors –				
due within				
one year	(149)		(147)	
Net current				
assets		28		20
Total assets				
less current				
liabilities		435		371
Creditors –				
due after				
more than				
one year		(91)		(133)
		344		238
Called-up				
share				
capital		44		44
Reserves		300		194
		344		238

The same balance sheet may be published using a different format:

Balance sheet at 30 June 199-

	199- £m	199- £m
Assets employed		
Fixed assets	407	351
Current assets	177	167
Total assets	584	518
Creditors due within		
one year	(149)	(147)
Net current assets		
(and liabilities)	28	20
Total assets less current		
liabilities	435	371
Financed by		
Creditors due after more		
than one year	91	133
Called-up share capital	44	44
Reserves	300	194
Total capital and reserves	344	238
	435	371

The differences between the two formats are that in the second one:

- Creditors due after one year – is moved to the lower 'half' of the balance sheet
- Net current assets – is listed as an extra, or 'memorandum', line into the layout of balance sheet.

Fixed assets

These include land, buildings, plant, equipment, fixtures and fittings. Fixed assets are stated at cost, less accumulated depreciation, or may be included at a professional valuation in the case of land and buildings.

Consider an asset purchased for £120,000 on 1 October 199-, with an estimated useful life of five years and a residual value assessed at £20,000. The depreciation is 20 per cent a year of:

Purchase cost of £120,000
less
Estimated residual value of £20,000
equals
Depreciation of £20,000 per annum.

At 30 September 199- + 3 years, the net book value of the asset will be:

	£'000
Cost	120
Aggregate depreciation	
(3 years × 20)	60
Net book value	60

Current assets

These consist of:

- raw materials and finished goods, stocks, plus work-in-progress
- debtors – i.e. amounts owed to the company by clients or customers
- deposits and short-term investments
- cash.

Creditors due within one year

These consist of:

- short-term borrowings, such as overdrafts. (A bank overdraft may seem a surprising item because it could be a regular feature of the balance sheet each year. This does not matter, however, since a bank overdraft is usually re-negotiable annually and repayable on demand – so it is a creditor falling due within one year)

- current instalments of loans
- other creditors, e.g. amounts owed by the company to suppliers, to share-holders (dividends), and the Inland Revenue.

Net current assets

These are current assets less creditors due within one year.

Creditors due after more than one year

These usually consist mainly of:

- secured and unsecured loans, for example a bank loan repayable after say four years
- obligation under finance leases for the purchase of fixed assets.

Called-up share capital

This consists of ordinary, and in some cases, preference shares as well; both valued at nominal value. Share options are excluded until the shares are actually allotted to directors and staff.

Reserves

These consist of:

- retained profits

and, where appropriate,

- share premium account
- property revaluation.

Each of these items is explained below:

(1) *Retained profits*

These are all of the profits retained in the company since its formation (after the payment of corporation tax and dividends) to provide additional finance.

(2) *Share-premium account*

This is the total of the premiums received in excess of the nominal value for all shares issued at higher than nominal value, after deducting the expenses of issuing them, e.g. when shares are issued as purchase consideration for an acquisition or where additional shares are issued during the life of a company to pay for companies acquired and to raise additional capital, perhaps by way of a rights issue to existing shareholders.

Consider a rights issue of one for two with an issued and paid up share capital of £300,000 and the cash received by the company is £2.50 per share, net of expenses, compared with the nominal value of £1 per share.

- The number of shares issued will be 150,000.
- The called-up share capital will increase by £150,000 from £300,000 to £450,000.
- The cash received will be

  $150,000 \times £2.50 = £375,000.$

- The assets will increase by £375,000.
- A share premium of £225,000 will arise,

  i.e. £375,000 cash received

less
£150,000 additional capital issued.

- This will be shown on the other side of the balance sheet under reserve.

(3) *Property revaluation*

This is the increase in value over the figure included in the balance sheet arising from a professional valuation of land and buildings by a qualified property surveyor.

Real-life balance sheets often present more detailed information. A familiarity with the basic layout of a balance sheet, however, means that the detailed balance sheet is just as easy to understand. Some other items which might arise include:

(1) *Intangible assets*

A small, but growing, number of companies include in the balance sheet a valuation of intangible assets (see definition on page 54). For example, in respect of brand names acquired by the purchase of businesses from other companies, the accounting policy adopted by Grand Metropolitan for including brands in the balance sheet, is that significant owned brands, acquired after 1 January 1985, the value of which is not expected to diminish in the foreseeable future, are recorded in the balance sheet as fixed intangible assets. No depreciation is provided on these assets but their value is reviewed annually and the cost written down as an exceptional item where permanent diminution in value has occurred.

(2) *Investments*

These might consist of:

- Investments in related companies, with a shareholding of between 20 and 50 per cent, which are say valued at the cost of the shares, less goodwill written off on acquisition, plus the investor company's share of retained profits and reserves since the date of acquisition.
- Investments in other companies which are valued individually at the lower of cost or net realizable value. For listed shares, net realizable value is the market value of the shares. For unlisted shares, e.g. in a private company, net realizable value is estimated by the directors.

(3) *Stocks*

These might consist of:

- raw materials and consumables
- work-in-progress
- finished goods and goods for resale.

Stocks are valued at the lower of cost or net realizable value. Interest is not usually included but, where appropriate, cost includes production and other direct overhead expenses.

(4) *Debtors*

These are primarily trade debtors, i.e. relating to amounts owed by customers.

(5) *Other creditors (due within one year)*

These can consist of:

- trade creditors, i.e. relating to

amounts owed to suppliers
- corporation taxation
- ordinary dividend payable
- current-year obligations under finance leases for the purchase of assets.

(6) *Provisions for liabilities and charges*
Obligations such as payments to the staff pension scheme and deferred taxation.

(7) *Special reserve*
This is an item not commonly encountered. It might be described as a technical adjustment to the balance sheet. It could arise where the share premium account has been reduced by a transfer to an undistributable special reserve, following a special resolution passed by shareholders and confirmed by court order.

(8) *Related companies' reserves*
is a Group's share of the reserves of related companies.

(9) *Minority shareholders' interests*
is the value of that part of subsidiary companies owned by minority shareholders directly in the subsidiary, rather than by a Group.

Goodwill

Goodwill merits an explanation although it is encountered only occasionally on a balance sheet. On the acquisition of a business, where the price paid exceeds the value of the net assets acquired, then the difference is treated as goodwill. Many companies write off goodwill against the reserves in the year of acquisition and so it does not appear on the balance sheet.

Research and development

Research and development is an item which occurs infrequently on a balance sheet, because most companies write off the expenditure in the year in which it is incurred as a charge to the profit and loss account, rather than capitalise it as an asset on the balance sheet.

Source and application of funds statement

UK companies are required to publish a source-and-application-of-funds statement annually, in addition to a profit and loss account and balance sheet.

The source and application of funds statement shows:

- the source of funds generated, e.g.:
  - profit before tax
  - share issues.
- the use of funds applied, e.g.:
  - purchase of fixed assets
  - increased stocks
  - increased debtors
  - tax and dividends paid.

The source and application of funds statement is somewhat complicated to understand for non-accountants. Cash-flow statements and forecasts are more helpful to business executives to help them with short-term cash management and control. None the less, source and application of funds statements are used by accountants for financial planning beyond the current financial year.

3. Ratio analysis

The range of ratio analyses and their uses is examined under the headings *performance ratios* and *stock-market ratios*.

(a) Performance ratios

These ratios can be broken down as follows:

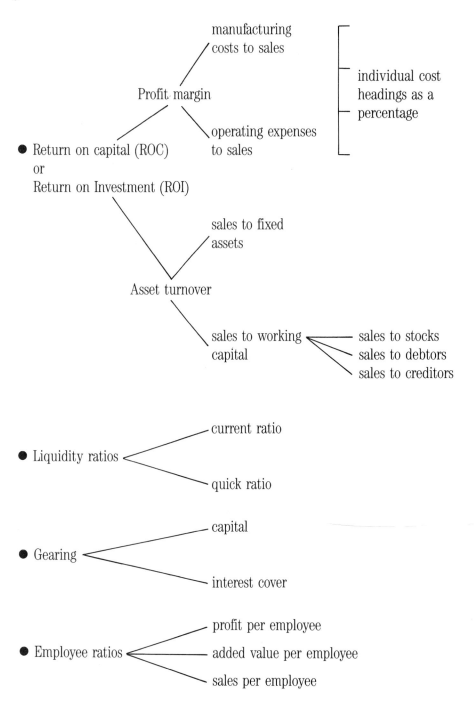

Some business executives regard ratio analysis as the preserve of accountants. Nothing could be more wrong. Ratio analysis is an essential tool for managers and can either indicate the extent of the financial well-being of a business or give an early warning of an unsatisfactory trend. Ratio analysis can be used to:

- assess the current performance of a business, on a monthly basis
- evaluate the acceptability of the budget proposed for the next financial year
- compare performance of subsidiaries and divisions within a group
- compare performance with that achieved by competitors, on an annual basis.

The first step is to understand the definition of the various ratios used to evaluate business performance, and the significance of each one.

Return on investment

The key yardstick of financial performance within a business is the return on investment achieved, and it is usually measured annually.

The basic definition is simple:

Per cent return on investment =

$$\frac{\text{Profit}}{\text{The amount invested to produce the profit}} (\times 100)$$

(Sometimes ROI is used as an abbreviation for return on investment.)

What happens in practice can be thoroughly confusing to non-accountants.

Different definitions of profit and investment are used by different companies, and as a result different terms may be encountered such as 'return on capital employed' (ROCE) and 'return on operating assets' (ROA).

Fortunately, there is an easy way to cut through this confusion: ask one of the finance staff in your company to explain the definition they have adopted. Some accountants will debate the merits of their particular definition at length. When used to evaluate performance within a group or company, however, the most important features are that the definition adopted is:

- easily understood by both managers and finance staff
- used in a consistent way by each division and subsidiary

because there is no consensus among qualified accountants in general of a correct definition of return on investment.

None the less, it is helpful to know the alternative definitions most commonly used for profit and investment when used in connection with return on investment.

Profit is usually defined as either profit before interest and tax, or as profit before tax.

Investment may be defined as:

- the capital employed as shown on the balance sheet, i.e. the fixed and current assets employed in the business minus all of the liabilities or
- the operating assets employed, namely: fixed assets, plus current assets, less creditors due within one year, excluding bank overdrafts and other borrowings.

Clearly, the percentage return on investment figures calculated for a particular company may differ significantly depending upon the definitions chosen for profit and investment. For the purpose of comparison within a company, however, it is worth stressing that it is the changes and differences in the ratios which are of prime importance.

Freehold land and building valuation

In the balance sheet of a listed company, the valuation of freehold land and buildings will probably be updated at least every five years, in order to avoid a significant understatement of asset values. For a private company, if the freehold property is not needed as security for bank loans, the valuation in the balance sheet may be left at the original purchase cost of, say, over 20 years ago. The only reference to this undervaluation in the Annual Report may be an item in the Directors' Report stating that the current market value is greater than the figure shown in the balance sheet.

By calculating a return on investment on this undervalued freehold basis, however, the owners may be fooling themselves that the return on investment is satisfactory, when it is not. Consider the following example:

Per cent return on operating assets (ROA)

$$= \frac{\text{Profit before interest and tax}}{\text{Operating assets employed}}$$

$$= \text{say, } \frac{\text{\£264,000}}{\text{\£1.2m}}$$

= 22 per cent, based on balance sheet valuation

If the value of the freehold property is understated by, say, £800,000, then on a current-valuation basis:

Per cent return on operating assets (ROA)

$$= \frac{\text{\£264,000}}{\text{\£1.2m} + \text{\£0.8m}}$$

= 13.2 per cent, based on current freehold valuation

Acceptable level of return on investment

It is a step forward to understand the calculation of return on investment, but this does not answer the important question, 'What is an acceptable percentage return?'

Clearly the percentage return on investment should exceed:

● the percentage return achievable from a relatively risk-free investment such as a major building society, expressed grossed up for income tax at the standard rate – because otherwise a better return could be achieved simply by investing the money and receiving the interest
● the cost of overdraft interest – because otherwise the return achieved does not cover the borrowing cost of the investment.

In practice, however, an acceptable return on investment should be significantly higher than the above to provide an adequate reward for the risks involved and the management expertise required.

Many stock-market-listed companies regard an acceptable return on operating assets, calculated using profit before interest and tax, to be a minimum of 20 per cent. More importantly, however, these companies would regard 25 per cent as a realistic goal to be achieved.

An analysis of return on investment

To manage the return on investment may seem to call for the ability to juggle simultaneously two completely different aspects of a business, profit and the funds invested. What is more, it may appear just as difficult to do as juggling, not two, but seven balls at once.

Fortunately, return on investment can be broken down into two separate and more easily manageable aspects of business:

Return on investment

$$= \frac{\text{Profit before tax and interest}}{\text{Assets employed}}$$

$$= \frac{\text{Profit before tax and interest}}{\text{Sales turnover (or fee income)}} \times \frac{\text{Sales turnover}}{\text{Assets employed}}$$

$$= \text{Per cent profit margin on sales} \times \text{Assets turnover}$$

So the key to improving the return on investment is to increase:

● either the per cent profit margin on sales
● or the asset turnover
● or, better still, both of these.

To do any of these may seem almost as daunting as the apparent juggling needed to improve the return on investment. This is not so. Both the profit margin on sales and the asset turnover can be broken down into more easily manageable parts.

Profit margin on sales

The items which determine the per cent profit margin on sales are:

Sales turnover or fee income
less
Cost of sales
equals
Gross profit
less
departmental overhead costs, including depreciation charges where these occur (e.g. marketing, sales, research and development, production, distribution, finance, administration)
equals
Profit before interest and tax.

Profit before interest and tax

So it becomes obvious that effective management and control of the percentage profit margin on sales requires attention to:

● The percentage gross profit achieved, i.e. gross profit expressed as a percentage of sales turnover, and
● The percentage of departmental costs, i.e. departmental costs experienced as a percentage of sales turnover.

The percentage profit before interest and tax on sales turnover tends to vary widely with the nature of the business. For construction companies it may be as low as between 2 and 4 per cent. For food supermarkets and some wholesale businesses it may be between 3 and 5 per cent. At the other extreme, some service companies may achieve more than 15 per cent. Many businesses achieve less than 10 per cent profit before interest and tax on sales turnover.

So every decimal point of percentage profit margin is important. For example, consider a business with an annual sales turnover of £10 million and the following budgeted cost for 199-:

199- Budget	*£m*	*%*
Sales turnover	10.00	100
Cost of sales	3.88	38.8
Gross profit	6.12	61.2
Marketing	0.63	6.3
Sales and customer		
* service*	2.37	23.7
Distribution	0.90	9.0
Development	0.93	9.3
Finance and		
* administration*	0.47	4.7
Profit before interest		
* and tax*	0.82	8.2

During the year assume that the gross profit falls from 61.2 to 60.3 per cent, i.e. a decrease of only 0.9 percentage points. One response is to regard a gross profit of more than 60 per cent as a figure that many businesses would envy. This would be totally unacceptable to the profit-driven manager. Assuming that departmental overhead costs remain the same percentage of turnover as budgeted, this means that the profit margin will fall from 8.2 to 7.3 per cent, i.e. a similar decrease of 0.9 percentage points. On a sales turnover of £10m, the profit before interest and tax will fall by £90,000 from

£820,000 to £730,000.

Now consider a situation where:

● the actual sales turnover falls to £9.5m compared with budgeted sales of £10m
● the cost of sales remains at the budgeted level of 38.8 per cent
● total overheads are allowed to remain at the budgeted amount of £5.3m.

Whereas the total overheads were budgeted to be 53 per cent of sales turnover, if the overheads remain at £5.3m, these become 55.8 per cent of the reduced sales turnover of £9.5 million. So the profit margin will fall by a similar amount from 8.2 to 5.4 per cent, because then overheads have increased by 2.8 percentage points. Profit before interest and tax will fall from £820,000 to £540,000.

So a clear message is evident. Whenever sales turnover falls, every effort must be made to reduce overhead levels as much as possible to offset partially the loss of profit, while avoiding lasting damage to the infrastructure of the business.

Asset turnover

The concept of managing asset turnover is likely to be less familiar to many managers than managing the profit margin on sales. It makes the point, however, that every pound of assets invested in the business must be made to work, or better still to 'sweat', to achieve the highest level of sales possible.

What does this mean in practical terms? Consider a hotel, with a ballroom that is used only in the evening for dinner dances and banquets. A relatively modest investment in moveable partitions may allow the room to be used for conferences of various sizes during the day. The introduction of either a 'twilight shift' in the evenings or a seven-days-a-week 'continental shift' may allow for increased sales and asset turnover to be achieved from expensive production facilities. Equally, when new investment is being incurred to equip a new retail sales unit or to install costly production equipment, speed is essential. The aim must be to bring the facilities into use as soon as possible in order to increase asset turnover. Unused floor space, whether owned or rented, is costly. The action to be taken will depend upon how long the space is likely to remain unused. Possible action includes either subletting unused space on a short-term basis or relocating part of the business to allow a complete building to be let or sold.

Working capital must be used just as productively as investment in fixed assets. The main elements of working capital are stock and work-in-progress; debtors (cash owed to the business by customers) and creditors (cash owed by the business). Some managers believe that stock and work-in-progress levels, debtors and creditors are the responsibility of the finance function in the business. This is nonsense. Managers must exercise their accountability to manage these elements of working capital, with the assistance of finance staff.

Separate ratios need to be calculated for:

- stock and work-in-progress
- debtors
- creditors.

Each one is defined and explained as follows:

Stock Ratios

Stock ratios are usually expressed in one of two ways:

- either the number of days of stock and work-in-progress held
- or the number of times stock and work-in-progress is turned over annually.

The calculations are:

Stock turnover (days) =

$$\frac{\text{Average stock and work-in-progress during year}}{\text{Annual cost of sales}} \times 365$$

(Annual) stock turnover =

$$\frac{\text{Annual cost of sales}}{\text{Average stock and work-in-progress during year}}$$

It may seem surprising that the annual cost of sales is used to calculate stock turnover rather than annual sales. The reason is simply to compare like with like, because stock values and cost of sales are calculated on the same basis.

Consider the following example:

	£m
Annual sales	10.00
Cost of sales	3.88
Gross profit	6.12
Stock and work-in-progress:	
at beginning of year	1.87
at end of year	2.21
Average stock and work-in-progress	2.04

Stock turnover (days)

$$= \frac{\text{Average stock and work-in-progress}}{\text{Annual cost of sales}}$$

$$= \frac{\pounds2.04 \text{ million}}{\pounds3.88 \text{ million}} \times 365 = 192 \text{ days}$$

(Annual) stock turnover

$$= \frac{\text{Annual cost of sales}}{\text{Average stock and work-in-progress}}$$

$$= \frac{\pounds3.88 \text{ million}}{\pounds2.04 \text{ million}} = 1.9 \text{ times}$$

Of the two methods commonly used, the stock turnover in days is probably more meaningful for managers. If in the following year, the value of stock and work-in-progress were to increase from 192 days to, say 199 days, it is obvious that it has taken an extra week to turn inventory into sales. The corresponding change in annual stock turnover from 1.9 times to 1.83 times is less revealing.

In a manufacturing compay with a large investment in inventory, it may make sense to calculate separate ratios for:

- raw materials
- work-in-progress
- finished goods ready for sale

in order to identify where corrective action is most needed.

Debtor ratio

On an annual basis, this is usually calculated by:

Debtor ratio =

$$\frac{\text{Debtors at year end}}{\text{Annual sales}} \times 365 \text{ (number of debtor days)}$$

On a monthly basis, this is often calculated on an equivalent number of days. For example, consider this calculation of the debtor ratio for June 1989:

Value of outstanding debtors
at end of June   = £130,000
Invoiced sales – June   = £57,000
           – May   = £63,000
           – April   = £50,000

Outstanding debtors of £130,000 is equivalent to sales in:

June of £57,000 = 30 days
May of £63,000 = 30 days
April of £10,000 = $\frac{6 \text{ days}}{66 \text{ days}}$ (pro rata to month of sales of £50,000)

Every business, regardless of size, should monitor the number of debtor days outstanding each month. An increase of only a single day during a month requires immediate corrective action. Consider the impact of an increase in debtor days outstanding for a relatively small business with an annual sales turnover of £3.65m, i.e. sales of £10,000 a calendar day. Assume that the average number of debtor days is allowed to increase by seven days throughout the financial year, i.e. customers are allowed an extra week to pay their invoices. The effect is significant on both the bank overdraft and the amount of profit:

- The bank overdraft will increase by £70,000 (because an extra seven days' sales, at £10,000 per day, will remain unpaid)

- the additional overdraft interest on additional borrowings of £70,000 for a year at, say, 14 per cent interest will be almost £10,000 a year.

In a business with significant export sales, which may take considerably longer to be paid for, there is a case for calculating each month the debtor days separately for:

- home sales
- export sales
- total sales.

Creditor ratio

On an annual basis, this is usually calculated by:

Creditor ratio

$$= \frac{\text{Creditors at year end}}{\text{Annual purchases}} \times 365$$

= no. of creditor days

On a monthly basis, this is often calculated on the basis of an equivalent number of days, in the same way as for debtors. By knowing the number of days of credit being taken from suppliers, it enables a manager to ensure that the policy of payment to suppliers is being adhered to, in overall terms.

Liquidity ratios

The survival of a business depends upon the ability to pay creditors acceptably soon enough. Liquidity ratios indicate the ability to pay creditors due within one year sufficiently quickly. There are two types:

- current ratio
- quick ratio.

Current ratio

A commonly used definition is:

Current ratio =

$$\frac{\text{Current assets}}{\text{Creditors due within a year,}}$$
excluding borrowings

Current assets are primarily stocks, work-in-progress, debtors, cash-in-hand and any other liquid resources. The current assets represent the cash tied up in the business, but which is continually circulating. In a manufacturing company, raw materials are purchased, then pass through the work-in-progress stage during the production process, become finished goods, i.e. stock for sale, are turned into debtors when the sale is invoiced and finally produce cash when the customer pays. The cycle starts again when some of the cash is used to purchase more raw materials.

Clearly, the current assets should comfortably exceed the value of creditors due for payment within a year to ensure that invoices can be paid sufficiently promptly. If the current assets were only to equal the creditors due within a year, then some increase in borrowings would probably be needed, simply because some of the current assets are tied up in stocks and work-in-progress, so will take longer to be turned into cash.

One rule of thumb which is used is that the current ratio of a healthy business should be at least 2.0, in order to provide an adequate safety margin to ensure that invoices can be paid sufficiently quickly. It has to be said, however, that many large and successful companies, with adequate unused borrowing facilities, operate on a current ratio much nearer to 1.0 than 2.0.

Quick ratio
A commonly used definition is:

Quick ratio =

$$\frac{\text{Current assets, excluding stock and work-in-progress}}{\text{Creditors due within one year}}$$

This means that the 'cash and near-cash' resources, i.e. debtors, cash-in-hand and any other liquid assets, are being compared with outstanding invoices which need to be paid.

If the ratio is less than 1.0, then the implications may be:

- additional borrowings will be needed to pay creditors sufficiently quickly, or
- extended credit will have to be taken, with the likelihood of court action for non-payment of invoices and the withholding of deliveries by suppliers
- the business requires an injection of capital to finance the present scale of operations adequately.

None the less, some businesses do manage to survive for a surprisingly long time with a quick ratio significantly below 1.0. It has to be said, however, that the important word is 'survive'. Such a warning signal should not be ignored.

Gearing ratio

The gearing ratio shows the percentage of borrowed money in relation to the shareholders' funds in the company. A commonly used definition is:

Gearing ratio =

$$\frac{\text{Net borrowings}}{\text{Shareholders' funds}} \times 100 \text{ per cent}$$

(= percentage gearing)

Net borrowings are bank loans and overdrafts, minus cash-in-hand and other liquid resources.

Shareholders' funds are represented by the balance-sheet valuation of the shareholders' funds invested in the company. These are then issued as paid-up share capital, at nominal value, plus accumulated reserves. The reserves are the profit retained in the business since it was formed, plus any property-revaluation surplus and share-premium account value where appropriate.

These are occasions when even companies listed on a stock-market have a gearing ratio in excess of 100 per cent. This means that lenders are providing more finance to operate the business than the shareholders. Indeed, there have been notable instances where listed companies have had a gearing ratio in the region of 250 per cent – temporarily! This may have resulted from a major acquisition which involved a large amount of borrowing to pay for it. In these circumstances, however, it is likely that the Chairman's statement in the Annual Report will state what has already been done, and what more will be done, to reduce the level of gearing substantially. Indeed, it may be necessary to sell some businesses in order to reduce the gearing sufficiently quickly to an acceptable level.

The consequence of a high gearing ratio is a heavy burden of loan and overdraft interest charged to the profit-and-loss account. When the economic climate deteriorates, there may well be a compound effect on profit. Not only are trading profits likely to fall, but interest rates could increase as well.

One way of calculating the effect of gearing upon profit is to calculate the interest cover, which is commonly defined as:

Interest cover =

$$\frac{\text{Profit before interest and tax}}{\text{Interest payable}} \text{ (number of times)}$$

A rule of thumb, and one which should not be ignored because the cost may be a loss of financial prudence, is that the interest cover should be at least 4.0, and preferably 5.0 or more using the above definition.

Employee ratios

Some businesses use various employee ratios as a measure of productivity, especially during periods of rapid expansion when productivity may fall in the pursuit of growth. Ratios commonly used include:

- *sales per employee* – but this could be maintained or increased as a result of a higher 'bought-in material' or 'sub-contracted' content of sales
- *added value per employee* – added value eliminates the possible distortion of any differences in the bought-in and subcontracted content by deducting these from sales
- *profit before tax per employee* – which can be highly revealing.

In professional partnerships, useful employee ratios include:

- average fee income per professional staff person
- average fee income per equity partner
- average profit before tax per equity partner

For example, consider a professional partnership with:

Annual fee income	= $5.6m
Total fee earners	= 50
Number of equity partners	= 10
Profit before tax	= $960,000
Average fee per fee earner	= $112,000 ($5.6m/50)
Average fee income per equity partner	= $560,000 ($5.6m/10)
Average profit before tax per equity partner	= $96,000 (960,000/10)

Another useful ratio to manage in a professional partnership is the professional staff support ratio, defined as:

Professional staff support ratio

$$= \frac{\text{Total number of professional staff}}{\text{Total number of other staff}}$$

To maintain profitability, any increase in this ratio must be adequately justified and not allowed to happen by accident or indulgence.

Indexation

When analysing trends in the performance of a company over five years or more, then even inflation of between 5 and 10 per cent a year distorts the picture significantly. One method of analysis is to index the figures using a base of 100 for the first year;

then to adjust subsequent years' figures using the movement in the appropriate index, such as the retail price index.

Using ratio analysis

Some managers want to know what is a 'good' or 'correct' figure for a particular ratio. This misses the essence of ratio analysis. For example, a 'nil' gearing ratio (indicating no borrowings at all) could be 'bad' rather than 'good'. It could reflect the fact that profitable opportunities have not been pursued because of an excessively conservative dislike of any borrowings.

As has been stated previously, some ratios differ widely according to the nature of the industry. The profit margins in the construction industry are likely to be dramatically lower than those of companies supplying luxury goods, as a generalization. Within a particular company, it is the trends which are of most importance. For example ratio analysis reveals whether productivity and profitability are declining in the pursuit of rapid growth.

Comparisons with competitors

Ratio analysis provides the opportunity to compare the performance of a company with that of competitors. Simply to obtain a copy of the published accounts of competitors and to calculate the ratios may produce some surprising contrasts, and some equally misleading figures because:

- profit may be calculated on a different basis
- balance sheets may be valued on a different basis.

Some examples will make the point emphatically. Consider the treatment of staff-pension schemes. The present rules are contained in the Standard Statement of Accounting Practice number 24, commonly referred to as SSAP 24. Traditionally, the charge made in the profit and loss account has been the contribution to the pension scheme made by the company in the year. After several years of high investment returns, many companies have built up 'a surplus' in the pension funds. The assets accumulated now exceed the liabilities to be met. SSAP 24 provides a choice of accounting treatment to deal with a pension surplus:

- either the surplus can be added to the reserves in the balance sheet, e.g. Williams Holdings added £72m to the reserves in their 1988 balance sheet
- or the surplus can be taken to reduce the pension costs charged in the profit and loss account during the remaining service of employees to retirement. By choosing this option, Reed once increased the profit by £17m in a set of its accounts.

Other significant differences in balance-sheet treatment exist. A company may have revalued property assets this year. A competitor may not have revalued property for four years. The accounting rules allow brand names which are purchased, but not those created by a company, to be valued in the balance sheet. A small but growing number of companies now include a valuation of brand names purchased as part of a company acquisition in their balance sheets.

As a generalization, an experienced

accountant is needed to 'guestimate' the various adjustments needed to be made to published accounts for any worthwhile comparisons and conclusions to be made. Recognizing this difficulty, in some trade associations the members submit their results in a standardized format to a major firm of chartered accountants in order for ratios to be circulated to the participants on an anonymous basis. Another source of useful information may be an inter-company ratio comparison available from a commercial publisher on selected business sectors.

(b) Stock-market ratios

These can be broken down as follows:

- gross dividend yield
- dividend cover
- earnings per share
- price-earnings ratio
- market capitalization
- net asset backing.

It would be understandable for a person working on subsidiary or a division of a stock-market-listed company to consider that stock-market ratios are irrelevant to his or her job. The owner of a private company may take a similar view. Both would be equally wrong, for different reasons.

People working in stock-market-listed companies need to know the yardsticks by which the performance of their company is judged, and the consequences for inadequate results, namely the real threat of being taken over, and the risk of substantial job losses.

For an owner of a private company, a knowledge of stock-market ratios is needed to understand the performance required if it is decided to obtain a stock-market listing, or to take a realistic view of the amount an acquirer may pay to purchase the company.

At first sight, even the names of the various ratios seem complicated and daunting; gross dividend yield, dividend cover, earnings per share, price earnings ratio, market capitalization and net asset backing per share sound like a foreign language. The reality is totally different. Once explained these ratios are simple to understand and calculate. Each ratio will now be defined in turn, and then a worked example used to illustrate the calculation.

Gross dividend yield

The gross dividend yield is the return received by the shareholder by the receipt of a dividend, ignoring any deduction of income tax, calculated as a percentage of the current market price of the shares. The method of calculation is:

Gross dividend yield

$$= \frac{\text{Gross annual dividend per share}}{\text{Current market share price}}$$
(before deduction of income tax)

This is a different calculation from that for the gross percentage dividend, which is:

Gross percentage dividend

$$= \frac{\text{Gross annual dividend per share}}{\text{Nominal value of share}}$$

So an understandable reaction would be, why bother with an extra calculation? The answer is simple. The percentage dividend allows comparison only with the dividend paid by the same company in previous years. The gross dividend yield allows a meaningful comparison to be made of the relative dividend income to be received from the shares of different companies.

Dividend cover

The dividend cover is the number of times the profits, after tax earned for the ordinary shareholders, exceed or 'cover' the gross dividend paid. The method of calculation is:

$$\text{Dividend cover} = \frac{\text{Earnings}}{\text{Gross dividend paid}}$$

The word 'earnings' is shorthand for the profits after tax earned for the ordinary shareholder in the parent company, before extraordinary items.

The dividend cover may be regarded as an indication of the safety margin by which the earnings exceed the gross dividend. If the dividend cover is 1.0, this means that the whole of the earnings, i.e. profits after tax, has been used to pay the dividend to shareholders. If the dividend cover is less than 1.0, which sometimes happens, in effect the shareholders are being paid some of the capital value of their share disguised as a dividend. This may be a conscious decision by the board, faced with a disappointing profit for the year, as a show of confidence by maintaining the same dividend payment in pence per share as was made in the previous year. The message behind this decision is 'Don't worry; the setback will not be repeated next year'. What it does mean, however, is that the company may have had to increase the overdraft to maintain the dividend payment, and so has to start the financial year facing an increased interest charge to the profit and loss account.

The most important source of finance for any company is profit retained in the business, after paying corporation tax and an acceptable level of dividend to shareholders. A stock-market-listed company should aim to pay an adequate dividend yield and still be able to achieve a dividend cover greater than 2.0, i.e. more profit should be left in the company to finance business development and growth than is paid to shareholders by dividend.

Earnings per share

The earnings per share is expressed in pence, and is the earnings for the year divided by the weighted average number of shares in issue during the year. The method of calculation is:

$$\text{Earnings per share} =$$

$$\frac{\text{Earnings} \times 100}{\text{Weighted average number of issued shares}} \quad \text{(pence per share)}$$

A key measure of profitability for a stock-market-listed company is the growth in earnings per share, because it takes into account not merely trading profit from operations, but the effect of interest charges on profit and the overall level of corporation tax, so that the earnings are the total income earned from shareholders, and not just the amount of dividend paid, together with the ability to raise finance without issuing more ordinary shares.

Whenever additional shares are issued, for example

- by a rights issue (see below) to existing shareholders to finance expansion
- to pay for the acquisition of another company, instead of using cash
- to executives under a share-option scheme.

then the weighted average number of share issued increases, and unless the earnings increase by a similar proportion, the earnings per share will be reduced. The expression often used to describe this situation is 'a dilution in the earnings per share'.

Rights issue is an issue of shares for cash made to existing shareholders, pro rata to their existing holding of shares. For example, a 1 for 4 rights issue means that each shareholder is entitled to buy one additional share for every four already owned. In the case of a listed company, the shareholder has the opportunity to sell the rights rather than buy the additional shares, and would receive any surplus value of the market price for the shares compared with the rights-issue price.

The aim of a stock-market-listed company should be to maximize the growth in earnings per share throughout the medium and long term, without a reduction or setback in any year. The most successful companies listed on the stock-market have achieved compound annual growth in earnings per share of more than 20 per cent a year over a decade and longer.

Price-earnings ratio

Price-earning ratios, often referred to as PE ratios, are published daily in the *Financial Times* for stock-market-listed companies, along with the gross dividend yield, dividend cover and other information about the share of each company. The method of calculation is what the name suggests:

Price-earnings ratio

$$= \frac{\text{Stockmarket share price}}{\text{earnings per share}}$$

The stock-market share price used is the one published in the financial newspapers at the close of business in the stock exchange for the previous evening.

If say, the average price-earnings ratio of a cross-section of several hundred companies was 12.9, this could be interpreted to mean that the share price of a typical company was 12.9 times the earnings per share achieved in the previous year.

As a generalization, when the price-earnings ratio of a company is higher than the average for other companies in the same business sector, the stock-market expects the company to achieve higher than average earnings per share in the foreseeable future to justify the above-average valuation of the shares. In certain circumstances, the explanation may be quite different. For example, a takeover bid for the company may be widely expected, and the share price has already increased significantly in anticipation of the price to be offered by the bidder.

It must never be forgotten that the analysis of share prices, and especially the prediction of future changes, cannot be done simply by calculating the various ratios. If this was possible, making a fortune on the stock-market would be easy. In practice, even the most experienced investment-fund managers make costly errors of judgement from time to time.

Market capitalization

The market capitalization of a stock-market-listed company is simply the total value placed upon the shares of the company. It is calculated by:

Market capitalization = number of issued shares × most recent share price

Of course, the market capitalization does not indicate the price a takeover bidder would have to pay to acquire the company. Typically, even if a rival bidder does not make an increased bid, an offer of about 35 per cent more than the share price when the offer was first anticipated may be needed for a successful bid. In a contested-bid situation, a successful bid may require to be at least 50 per cent more than the previous price of the shares.

Net asset backing

The net asset backing is usually expressed in pence per share and is the balance sheet worth of each share. It is calculated by:

Net asset backing =

$$\frac{\text{Shareholders' funds in the balance sheet}}{\text{Number of issued shares}} \text{ (price per share)}$$

The shareholders' funds consist of the issued share capital, calculated at the nominal value, plus reserves. In addition to retained profits, the reserves include the share premium account and any property revaluation where appropriate.

Some people find it surprising that the net asset backing per share shown by the audited balance sheet of a company may be significantly higher or lower than the present market price of the shares. Once again, the reason is simple. For most companies the prime determinants of the market share price are the most recent earning per share and the expected future growth. Balance sheet asset values tend to have a major influence on the share price only when there is a substantial proportion of the share price in the form of available cash within the company and readily saleable freehold properties.

For a profitable company which is not capital intensive, such as a successful advertising agency, the net asset backing per share may be only a small proportion of the market price of the shares. In contrast, consider a manufacturing company with poor profitability and high asset backing per share in the balance sheet. The likelihood is that the assets could not be turned into a corresponding amount of cash, even by liquidating the company. So the market share price will be depressed by the poor profitability, and may well be significantly lower than the net asset backing per share shown by the balance sheet.

Worked example
Consider the share information for a (fictional) company that could appear in the *Financial Times*:

199-					Div.		Yield	
High	Low	Stock	Price	+ or −	Net	Cover	Gross	P/E
595	425	Hickbush Holdings 50p	558	−4	15.0	2.4	3.6	11.6

The information tells the reader that the:

- highest market share price to date in 1991 was 595p
- lowest market share price was 425p
- nominal value of each share is 50p
- share price at the close of business last evening was 558p (the average of the buying and selling prices)
- (average) share price was 4p lower than the previous evening
- total dividend paid on each share in the previous finance year was 15.0p, after the deduction of income tax at the standard rate of 25 per cent
- dividend cover in the previous year was 2.4 times the amount of dividend paid
- gross dividend yield in the previous year was 3.6 per cent
- price-earnings ratio is 11.6 at the most recent share price of 558p.

The calculation of these stock-market ratios for this fictional company would be based on the above data and on the following information taken from its Annual Report.

- gross dividend per share: 20p
- earnings: $412.0m
- gross dividend paid: $172.1m
- number of issued shares: 860.6m
- shareholders' funds in balance sheet: $3,438m

Gross dividend yield
(the per cent of current share price the investor receives as dividend)

$$= \frac{\text{Gross dividend per share}}{\text{Market share price}}$$

$$= \frac{20.0p}{558p}$$

$$= \textbf{3.6 per cent}$$

Dividend cover
(the number of times the profit attributable to the ordinary shareholder covers the dividend for the year)

$$= \frac{\text{earnings}}{\text{Gross dividend paid}}$$

$$= \frac{\$412.0m}{\$172.1m}$$

$$= \textbf{2.4 times}$$

Earnings per share
(the profit attributable to the ordinary shareholder earned in pence per share)

$$= \frac{\text{Earnings}}{\text{Weighted average number of issued shares}}$$

$$= \frac{\$412.0m}{860.6m}$$

$$= \textbf{48p per share}$$

Price-earnings ratio
(the number of years
required at last year's
earnings to equal the
market price of the share)

$$= \frac{\text{Stock-market share price}}{\text{Earnings per share}}$$

$$= \frac{558p}{48p}$$

$$= \textbf{11.6}$$

Market capitalization
(the aggregate value of the
ordinary shares at the
present market share price)

$= \text{Number of shares issued at year end} \times \text{market share price}$

$= 860.6m \times 558p$

$= \pounds4.8 \text{ billion}$

Net asset backing per share
(value of shareholders' funds
per ordinary share as shown
in the balance sheet)

$$= \frac{\text{Shareholders' funds in balance sheet}}{\text{Number of issued shares}}$$

$$= \frac{\pounds3,438m}{860.6m}$$

$$= \textbf{399p per share}$$

Comparative share performance

Occasionally, someone will ask 'What is a good price-earnings ratio?' as if to imply that there is a universal and everlasting benchmark to aim for. This misses the point completely. Consider the sharp fall in share prices that occurred in October 1987 and affected the stock-markets in many countries. The fall in share prices was more than 20 per cent in many cases, which means that price-earnings (PE) ratios fell by a similar percentage as a result, as the PE ratio is calculated by the most recent share price divided by the earnings per share. At any time, average PE ratios can differ significantly between the stock-markets of different countries. Equally, the PE ratios for different types of business on the same stock-market can vary widely.

The *FT*-Actuaries Share Indices table,
published daily in the *Financial Times*, gives the PE ratios and gross dividend yields for a variety of business sectors.

The most relevant comparisons to make for the shares of a particular company are with:

- the sector average in the *FT*-Actuaries Share Indices table
- broadly similar companies

Share value in private companies

Owners of private companies sometimes have extravagant and quite unrealistic views about the worth of their business if it were to be sold. The use of PE ratios gives a broad indication of the possible price an acquirer may be prepared to pay.

Consider a privately owned building materials company. Assume the profits before tax in 1990 were £600,000, and an increase to £650,000 is forecast for 199-. The net assets of the business, taking into account the present value of the freehold property, is £2.4m. The owners believe the business is worth at least £5m.

Valuation of private companies using PE ratios is usually done on the assumption that a full 35 per cent corporation tax should be deducted from the profits before tax to calculate the earnings.

Actual profit before tax	£600,000
Less 35 per cent corporation tax	(£210,000)
Earnings	£390,000

Say the PE ratio of the building materials sector was 10.8. The forecast profit growth for 199- is roughly 'average', so one could assume the average PE ratio would be used by a takeover bidder. Wrong! The evidence is that many buyers of private companies look for a discount on a comparable PE ratio for stock-market-listed companies of at least 20 per cent. This would suggest a PE ratio of about 8.6 times the earnings of £390,000, which is less than £3.5m.

It must be stressed, however, that PE ratios give only a broad indication of the likely purchase price for a private company. Other factors will influence the purchase price to be obtained. Factors which tend to increase the purchase price include:

- scarcity or rarity value, resulting from a shortage of attractive companies available to purchase in the sector
- a market leader in a niche business
- additional profit opportunities to be gained by the acquirer.

Factors which are likely to reduce the purchase price include:

- undue dependence on one customer
- low asset backing relative to the purchase price
- particular reliance on the personal contribution of the present owners, which may be difficult to replace.

6.2 Techniques to increase profits

The main techniques examined are:

- Budgetary control
- Cash management
- Profit management
- Financial analysis for decision-making.

1. Budgetary control

Sound budgets, prompt monthly reporting of actual results, and a regularly updated forecast of the results expected for the financial year are the essential foundations of financial management control.

Basic issues
First-class procedures are not sufficient to ensure effective budgeting and budgetary control. Suitable management attitudes are essential. These require two basic issues to be addressed:

(1) What level of achievement should the budget reflect?
(2) Who is responsible for achieving budgeted performance?

The budgeted level of performance should be demanding, but achievable by committed and co-ordinated management action.

It is not enough for the managing director, general manager, or a regional manager in charge of a separate business to be committed to the achievement of the budgeted profit. Nothing less than the collective cabinet commitment of the person in charge and each member of the team reporting directly to him or her is acceptable. Otherwise, people may adopt the parochial view that their only responsibility and concern is to achieve the sales or control the costs in line with their departmental budget. This would be nonsense, and must not be allowed to happen. For example, if the gross profit from sales falls below budget then every effort must be made to offset this by appropriate cost reduction throughout the business.

Budget assumptions

The assumptions on which the budget is to be constructed should be agreed by the executive team, and written down at the outset, to ensure that different departments do not make different assumptions and to ensure that the proposed budget can be reviewed by top management for changes required. Assumptions which need to be made and written down include:

- price increases for existing products and services
  - the proposed percentage increase and date to be implemented for each product or service group
- the date for the launch of each new product or service
- the dates planned for other events which will affect the budget such as:
  - new branch or store openings
  - relocation of premises
  - the appointment of additional distributors
- expected salary increases
- cost inflation for the various categories of expenditure
- currency exchange rates and commodity price movements, where appropriate
- the recruitment of additional staff
- major items of discretionary expenses within departmental budgets, such as marketing or research and development
- substantial capital expenditure projects
- impact of anticipated legislation and other external factors such as:
  - higher national insurance contributions
  - additional costs arising from, e.g. new requirements on food packaging.

Co-ordination

Most businesses are organised into numerous separate departments and functions. If detailed budgets are prepared by each department and then simply aggregated into an overall budget for the business, the resulting profit and cash flow may be unacceptable. Co-ordination at an early stage is needed to ensure this does not happen.

An effective way to achieve the co-ordination is by the executive directors of the business collectively preparing and agreeing an acceptable outline budget before the preparation of detailed departmental budgets is started. The outline budget needs to be no more than an outline profit-and-loss and cash-flow budget for the year. It means, however, that each director will know what departmental budget will be acceptable from the outset.

Sales budget

Ideally, the sales budget will be prepared and the implications for other departments discussed with them, before they need to start preparing their detailed budgets. Otherwise, departments such as purchasing, production, order processing and physical distribution will have to base their budgets upon a 'guestimate' of the volume and mix of sales to be budgeted.

Every effort must be made to budget sales as accurately as possible, despite the uncertainties involved. Any variance between budgeted and actual sales is likely to have a disproportionately greater effort on budgeted profit and cash flow.

Sales value should not merely be estimated as a total amount, but should be calculated from the number of units to be sold and the sales prices to be obtained.

Overhead costs

The annual budgeting exercise provides an opportunity not merely to budget departmental costs for the coming year but also to challenge the existence, size and methods of each department. Unfortunately, not enough companies seize the opportunity available.

It may sound like a recipe for anarchy, but it is not. The technique is known as *zero-based budgeting* and variations of it have been used for many years by some companies. In essence, it means adopting a blank piece of paper approach by considering how the need would best be served if the department did not exist at all. For example, perhaps physical distribution of goods would be subcontracted out completely rather than be provided by company-owned vehicles with a large number of staff employed. Or at least vehicles could be leased, instead of owned. The real benefits to be gained from zero-based budgeting arise from thinking about and challenging existing methods and standards.

Staff salaries, and the costs which inevitably occur as a result of employing staff, are a major part of most overhead-cost budgets. It is not adequate simply to budget a lump sum for staff costs. a detailed analysis needs to be budgeted month by month. Where additional staff are to be recruited during the budget year, each appointment should be specified in the following detail:

- job title
- salary and benefits
- date when employment will commence
- estimated capital expenditure required, e.g. company car, personal computer
- method and cost of recruitment

It is unacceptably sloppy to budget for additional staff on the naive assumption that each person will join on the first day of the financial year.

When departmental overhead budgets are reviewed by higher-level management, the list of additional staff proposed should be challenged critically. The need to terminate staff when sales fall significantly below budgeted levels is costly, painful, time-consuming and generally demotivating. The most effective way to avoid the problem is to take a hard-nosed approach to any excessive or premature staff recruitment proposed in a departmental budget.

In the same way all other overhead items should be budgeted accurately and supported by working papers which give the detail.

Large round sums for discretionary items such as trade exhibitions or press advertising should not be accepted. If a sum of, say, £150,000 is included in the budget, sufficient analysis must be provided, e.g. the exhibitions to be attended and the costs of each one. Press advertising should be detailed by the number of advertisments to be placed in each newspaper at an average cost per insertion.

Lump sums are equally unacceptable for items such as patent costs and overseas travel. The forecast cost for the current year, plus adjustments to reflect increased sales volumes and anticipated cost inflation is unsatisfactory as a basis for budgeting costs such as these. Patent costs need to be budgeted in terms of the number of applications to be made in each country, multiplied by the average cost expected in each country. Overseas travel needs to be budgeted on an estimated basis, based on who will need to travel to which countries and for how long.

Capital expenditure

Once again detail is required; a lump-sum approach is unacceptable.

Individual projects should be listed, and the total capital expenditure costs estimated for each one. Associated revenue costs connected with a project should be estimated, so that these are not omitted from the appropriate overhead-cost budget, e.g., the cost of additional software to be purchased with each personal computer. Equipment which needs to be replaced may be overlooked, e.g. the need for the existing telephone switchboard to be replaced by a larger one because the volume of calls can no longer be handled adequately.

The month in which each piece of capital expenditure will be invoiced by the supplier needs to be set out as part of the detailed budget. This may be thought excessive detail, but it is not. The combination of the proposed timing of capital expenditure and the differing working capital needs of the business during the year may exceed the borrowing facilities of the company. The only way to avoid this is to plan the capital expenditure on a month-by-month basis.

Every manager needs to realize that the inclusion of a particular project in an approved capital expenditure budget does not in any way automatically authorize the expenditure. Most companies rightly require a detailed commercial and financial justification to be presented and approved for all capital projects over a certain value. Equally, it is nonsense for a manager to be told during the budget year that a project will not be authorized because it was not itemized in the budget. Surely, if circumstances or priorities have changed, the manager should be allowed the proposed project provided that other capital expenditure items of a similar value are deleted.

The cash budget

For many types of business, cash is more difficult to budget accurately than profit. Even if actual sales are exactly in line with budget each month, there is no guarantee that customers will pay their invoices within the time allowed in the budget. Despite the inevitable inaccuracy, however, the most important budget of all is the cash budget. What is more, an annual cash budget is totally inadequate without additional detail. The cash budget must be calculated month by month, because there may be wide fluctuations during the year in the size of the overdraft required.

Every item of cash must be included such as:

- cash received from customers based upon the budgeted period of time to be allowed for payment by customers
- interest payable or receivable
- payments to trade customers – based upon a budgeted payment period from receipt of suppliers' invoices
- salaries and associated employment costs, such as pension and national insurance contributions
- capital expenditure, identified on a month-by-month basis.

Quarterly, six-monthly and annual outgoings need to be included, such as:

- rental and lease payments
- rates
- interim and final dividends
- advance corporation tax
- corporation tax
- insurance premiums
- bonus payments.

Monthly budget phasing

Obviously, to produce a monthly cash budget means that annual sales need to be budgeted on a month-by-month basis as well as operational costs and capital expenditure. This monthly analysis is often referred to as calendarizing or phasing the budget.

Sales need to be calendarized on a monthly basis as accurately as possible. Most businesses have seasonal fluctuations in sales, caused by a variety of factors. These must be taken into account. Fortunately, history may provide a reliable guide for monthly budget phasing of sales. A useful exercise is to calculate the percentage of annual sales which took place in each month of the three previous years. The pattern may be sufficiently similar to provide a reliable guide for the budget year.

Equally, the budgeted annual profit must be phased monthly in order to know whether or not the business is on course to achieve the budgeted profit quarter by quarter only, but this does not provide a sufficiently early warning of a profit shortfall.

Effective monthly reporting

Monthly reporting needs to be prompt. Information which is sufficiently accurate, but includes some estimated figures, should be produced within two weeks of the end of each monthly or four-weekly accounting period. After all, in the following month any estimates which were made can be adjusted to the actual figures. Some companies take four or five weeks to produce monthly results which is unacceptable.

Sales figures should be circulated daily,

weekly and monthly because these give an indication of likely performance against the budgeted profit.

With the widespread use of computers, managers tend to be inundated with figures and print-outs, but often lack sufficient useful information for management action. For example, a print-out of all debtors requires time spent identifying those customers where further action is needed to collect outstanding debts. To compound matters, some debtor print-outs include all customers who have made a purchase during the financial year, even if they do not owe any money at present.

Summary information which is particularly useful for management action includes:

- a list of customers with a debt outstanding for either 60 or 90 days, perhaps listed in decreasing order of size to focus immediately on the largest amounts
- a list of any customers who have been allowed to exceed their authorized credit limit.

Computer-produced graphics are a useful way of displaying a lot of data effectively. The capability to produce diagrams such as bar charts, pie charts and graphs is widely available with computers. Sadly, not enough accountants who are responsible for producing monthly reports in companies make sufficient use of the facility. If necessary, a manager should request the accountant to present information using graphics.

A set of monthly reports needs to be accompanied by a narrative which comments upon and explains significant items.

Without this the value of the figures is much reduced. When the monthly reports are to be reviewed at a board or management committee meeting, it is important that the reports and narrative are circulated in sufficient time for participants to have considered them before the meeting. Otherwise, not only is time likely to be wasted in the meeting but the discussion may well be unduly superficial too.

Monthly reporting should not be restricted to financial statements produced by the finance department. The information presented should be what is needed for the effective management of the business, and may include the value or number of:

- proposals or tenders submitted
- orders received
- employee numbers compared with budget
- sales lost through unavailability of stock.

Financial year forecasts

Once a budget has been authorized, any revision should be firmly resisted, even if the cause was either unforeseen or completely outside the control of the business, for example, an unexpected supplementary Budget by the government which increases the national insurance contributions payable by employers. Managers will always be keen to seek a revision which reduces the budgeted profit, but a request for an increase is unheard of. As soon as a budgeted profit is reduced, this immediately becomes an acceptable standard of performance. The original budget is quickly forgotten.

This must not be allowed to happen. For

a stock-market-listed company to explain a disappointing profit performance in terms of some subsidiaries failing to achieve budget would be unthinkable. It would be nothing less than an unacceptable and naive excuse. The management team must focus on the action to be taken to achieve the budgeted profit despite unforeseen setbacks.

Situations arise where during the early months of the year, the actual profit is in line with budget but events have already occurred which will adversely affect the remainder of the year. Examples include a reduction in the level of enquiries or orders received, an adverse change in currency exchange rates and bank interest levels, or an unexpected increase in raw material costs.

Forecasts of profit and cash flow for the full financial year should be updated regularly to quantify the shortfall expected. The year-end forecasts should be updated at least quarterly. Better still, the forecast should be reviewed monthly and amended whenever necessary. While the forecast will be prepared by the finance staff, it should be based upon discussions with the management team responsible for achieving it. Also, when a revised forecast is produced, it should be accompanied by a concise narrative to explain the changes and the reasons for them. The existence of a year-end forecast enables the board or management committee meeting to concentrate on what further action is to be taken to improve the forecast profit, rather than merely review the result for the previous month.

2. Cash management

A receiver or liquidator is appointed when creditors are not paid sufficiently promptly. At the time, the business may have made a small profit in the current month or the owners may feel confident that losses will be turned into profits during the next few months. The business may be expanding. All of this counts for nothing if creditors cannot be paid sufficiently quickly. Indeed, one of the causes of the problem may be that the business has been expanding too rapidly in relation to the amount of finance available.

It would be entirely wrong to give the impression, however, that cash management is needed only when a business might be facing receivership. Effective cash management is so important that every business should practise it 365 days a year, and to emphasize the point, 366 days each leap year.

Cash management is essential to optimize profit. Otherwise the amount of bank interest payable will be unnecessarily large. The finance staff do not manage the business, and neither do they manage cash. In both cases, they merely assist their colleagues in the management team. Cash management is a key executive task.

The foundation for effective cash management is a detailed cash-flow budget, calendarized month by month, as described already (see p. 83). The other essential ingredients of cash management include:

- ensuring the customers pay promptly
- planning and controlling the amount of money tied up in stock and work-in-progress
- paying creditors sufficiently quickly to avoid either commercial disadvantage or financial penalty

- making sure that the level of overhead costs is affordable
- ensuring that adequate finance and bank overdraft facilities are available
- regularly monitoring performance against the cash-flow budget
- maintaining a dialogue with the bank.

In addition, a prudent and rigorous approach is needed for capital expenditure decisions.

Debtor management

Debtor management is the entire process of obtaining prompt payment by customers. Some people imagine that all it involves is sending out invoices and writing reminder letters to customers who do not pay sufficiently quickly. If only it was that simple, but nothing could be further from reality. Some of the main elements of debtor management are:

Deposit with order

Whenever a custom-made product or service is supplied, a policy requiring a minimum deposit with the order should be considered. Such a policy should definitely be adopted, unless valid reasons exist which would damage the business. It is not necessarily a valid argument that none of your competitors has a similar policy. Many companies and professional partnerships have found a surprising willingness by customers to make an initial payment, especially when the amount of work involved is explained to them.

Interim invoicing

Many service businesses overlook valid opportunities for interim invoicing which should be agreed at the outset as a matter of routine. The aim should be to invoice the client as soon as each stage is completed.

Prompt invoicing

When goods are supplied to a customer, the use of a multi-part stationery automatically produces the invoice at the same time as the items are despatched. Substantial delay may occur, however, before a service is invoiced.

Creditworthiness

Invoicing promptly is important, but it assumes that the customer has the ability and intention to pay. The potential problems are when supplying some private companies and individuals.

The credit status of private companies should be checked. Simply to request references from two other suppliers may be inadequate. The customer may pay these two accounts promptly purely to have references available. Equally, a bank reference may not reveal sufficient information about the customer. Also, beware of the customer placing two or three small orders and paying them promptly, only to follow these with a large order without the ability or intention to pay. An up-to-date credit-status report on a company can be purchased for a few pounds. Obviously, credit-status checks should be used selectively, rather than as a matter of routine, as some businesses do. The message is clear, however – if in any doubt, obtain a credit-status report.

It is difficult to check the creditworthiness of an individual. Outward appearance may create the impression of wealth, but be nothing more than deliberate deceit. Cash with order should be requested or at least a worthwhile initial payment. A definite limit should be set for the maximum amount of credit to be allowed, and this should be strictly adhered to.

Credit limits

For many businesses, it makes sense to set a credit limit for each corporate customer, to establish the maximum credit which will be allowed at any time. Whenever the limit would be exceeded by supplying another order received, the appropriate manager should be alerted. One phone call requesting payment of some of the existing debt before the next order is completed may produce a cheque immediately.

Eliminating excuses

Some customers make a successful habit of waiting until they are pressed for payment to point out the omission of basic information on the invoice, such as:

- customer order number
- supplier's VAT number
- delivery address.

They will point out that until this information is provided, the invoice cannot even be accepted. Once again, the remedy is simple. Ensure that all the relevant order information, including the terms of payment, is clearly and accurately stated on the invoice.

Prompt-payment discount

In theory, a discount on the invoiced price which ensures prompt payment seems like a good idea. The reality may be quite different. Two issues need to be considered – the cost and the benefit.

Some companies offer a 2.5 per cent

discount for payment within seven days or ten days of the date of the invoice. If as a result a customer pays the invoice two months earlier than without such an incentive, then this is equivalent to an annualized cost of 15 per cent to the supplier. This is because a 2.5 per cent cost for receiving payment two months earlier must be multiplied by six to arrive at the annualized cost. When compared with the alternative cost of having a correspondingly large overdraft, this may appear reasonable in certain circumstances. If as a result of a 2.5 per cent prompt-payment discount, however, the customer pays only a month earlier, then the annualized cost to the supplier is 30 per cent, which is expensive.

Worse still, some large customers may pay their invoices after, say, a month and still automatically deduct the prompt-payment discount. Faced with this situation, some sales managers accept it rather than risk upsetting an important customer. This is far removed from effective cash management.

Requesting payment

On the day that payment becomes due, a request for payment should be made. A standard letter, produced by computer on flimsy paper with poor print quality and addressed simply to the accounts department, is almost certain to have no effect. It is likely to be regarded as junk mail and consigned immediately to the wastepaper bin.

When an order is accepted, the name, position and address of the person who will authorize payment should be established. In a multi-national company, invoices may need to be sent to a regional or head office located in another country. The request for payment should be addressed to the correct individual. It should ask that any reason why payment has not been made should be notified immediately. Telex or facsimile should be used rather than overseas airmail letters.

Telephone follow-up

If payment has not been received seven days from the first request for payment, a telephone call should be made to the person responsible for authorizing payment. If the response is unsatisfactory, the person who placed the order should be telephoned and asked to obtain payment without further delay. If any queries, reasons or excuses are raised to justify non-payment, these must be answered or dealt with immediately. Sometimes two or three weeks will be taken to answer a query, which is effectively granting extended credit to the customer as a result of administrative incompetence.

Further action

If payment is not forthcoming, further action should be taken within a matter of days. Delay or, more accurately, procrastination is likely to reduce significantly the chances of receiving payment at all. According to the amount and country concerned, either a debt-collecting agency or a solicitor should be instructed.

Stock and work-in-progress management

The cost of holding raw materials, production work-in-progress and finished goods ready for sale is alarmingly high. Various studies carried out by major companies have demonstrated that the annual cost of holding stock is between 25 and 40 per cent of the value of stock. In other words, every £1m of inventory costs between £250,000 and £400,000 a year to hold in stock.

At first sight, these figures seem difficult to believe. When the various elements of cost are identified, however, the reality becomes apparent. The cost of holding stock and work-in-progress includes:

- interest charges on the finance required
- occupancy costs such as rent, rates and any service charges for the premises
- heating and lighting of the premises
- insurance costs
- damage and theft of stock
- storage equipment and mechanical handling costs.

Effective inventory management requires continuous communication between marketing, sales, production and purchasing staff. In some companies, detailed production and purchasing budgets will be produced. One thing is certain, however, either the actual volume or mix of sales is likely to prove significantly different from the budget. This requires that:

- marketing staff alert the other departments to forthcoming promotional campaigns and the forecast impact on sales
- sales staff continuously notify both production and purchasing staff of changes in the volume of enquiries and orders received, so that schedules may be amended accordingly.

Every effort should be made to reduce the time of the production cycle to turn raw materials into finished goods for sale. The concept of just-in-time inventory management should be adapted by small businesses to get tangible results for themselves. These techniques are not the sole preserve of large companies.

Creditor payment

To delay paying creditors until legal action is commenced may be costly and counterproductive. For example, if tax is not paid by the date, the Inland Revenue will charge interest and it is not an allowable charge against taxable profits. Some suppliers will seize any opportunity to increase the price quoted in order to compensate themselves for anticipated slow payment. When a delivery or service is required urgently, the request for help from a slow-paying customer may be met with little enthusiasm.

The ingredients for effective supplier management and creditor payment include ensuring that:

- no order is placed without an agreed price. This happens surprisingly often, especially on urgent orders, and is an invitation to the supplier to choose the price to be paid
- each order is properly authorized
- payment is properly authorized. The order may have been supplied, but payment needs to be authorized to confirm that the quality and performance are satisfactory
- early payment is made to benefit from attractive discounts. The benefit to be gained by taking advantage of the prompt-payment discount may be substantially more than the cost of additional overdraft interest

- quantity discounts are taken for placing large orders, with the flexibility of changing call-off rates to suit varying demand. Some suppliers offer substantial percentage discounts for large orders. The negotiation of flexible call-off rates avoids the risk of excessive stocks if the demand is lower than expected
- the budgeted creditor-payment period is adhered to on an overall basis. If the budgeted credit payment is, say, 60 days, then this will be achieved by a selective approach to the speed with which each creditor is paid.

Overhead costs

A common cause of a cash-flow crisis is the creation of substantial overhead costs in anticipation of future sales, which do not result as quickly as expected. For example, the development of a major new product may be substantially more costly than expected and take considerably longer to achieve. Or the level of sales achieved from additional branches may be much lower than expected. It is not enough simply to produce a cash-flow budget based upon optimistic sales projections. It is essential to be satisfied that sufficient finance will be available if actual sales should be considerably lower than expected.

Another trap to be avoided is when the budget is based on an ambitious and continuously increasing sales pattern throughout the year. The staff required to achieve the budgeted sales growth need to be recruited and trained to make it happen. Caution is needed with recruitment elsewhere in the business, however, because if the sales growth is less than expected, the overhead burden will be a drain on both profit and cash flow.

Adequate finance

Cash flow is difficult to predict accurately. It depends not just on the volume and timing of sales during the year, but the speed with which customers pay their invoices as well.

Safety first must be the motto. It is dangerous, not merely unwise, to assume that the finance required is simply that indicated by translating an ambitious sales budget into a cash-flow requirement. If the actual sales fall below budget, there is likely to be a disproportionate effect on profit and cash flow. This applies particularly to service companies with overhead costs which are largely fixed in the short term over a wide range of sales levels, for example an insurance broker or an estate agent.

The cash-flow consequences of a lower level of sales must be quantified, and the board must be satisfied that adequate finance is available. The sources of external finance available include:

- issuing more 'paper' such as ordinary shares; preference shares; convertible loan stock; loan stock and loan notes
- sale and leaseback of freehold properties
- leasing and hire purchase of assets
- fixed-term loans
- debt factoring
- bank overdrafts.

Monitoring cash flow

It is not acceptable simply to check the bank statement each month to be satisfied that the balance is in line with the comparable figure in the cash-flow budget. The situation may be much worse than budget because:

- some major payments, such as VAT or property rents, were paid but not cleared for payment in time to appear on the month-end bank statement
- the finance staff have been slowing down payments to suppliers in order to keep within the cash-flow budget or overdraft limit
- a large unscheduled payment needs to be made next month.

The effective monitoring of cash flow requires each month:

- the actual receipts and payments to be compared with budget each month to identify differences which would otherwise remain hidden for a time
- the cash-flow forecast to be updated for each of the next three months and the remainder of the financial year in total to identify the need for corrective action.

In some large companies, the cash-flow forecast for the next month is prepared on a week-by-week basis for tight cash control.

Bank contact

Some companies mistakenly adopt the policy of avoiding contact with the bank manager wherever possible. This is short-sighted. Sooner or later, the time will come when the support of the bank is needed to help the business handle a temporary cash-flow crisis. When this happens, the goodwill created by regular communication with the bank is definitely helpful.

The minimum communication required is to telephone the bank if the overdraft limit is to be exceeded, even if only for a day. It is a basic courtesy and gives the confidence that the business knows what is happening to the overdraft. If the overdraft limit is likely to become inadequate, a meeting should be arranged to explain the circumstances and to present an up-dated monthly cash-flow forecast.

Other companies go further than this. The bank will be supplied with a copy of the audited accounts and the annual phased cash-flow budget and management accounts at intervals during the year. This is not essential. It does, however, give more confidence to the bank. It is possible, too, that the bank manager may be able to offer an alternative approach to meet the financing needs which is more attractive than an increased overdraft.

An example of the lay-out of a cash-flow forecast is given on page 92.

3. Profit management

Every manager must understand the anatomy of profit, but perhaps surprisingly the statutory or conventional profit and loss account is not sufficiently revealing about it. The profit and loss account needs to be analysed into variable and fixed costs, to show the marginal profit, for effective profit management.

Variable costs

Variable costs are those costs which increase or decrease directly pro rata to changes in sales volume. Examples of variable costs are:

- the materials used to make a product
- royalties payable on each sale

- carriage cost when using a parcels carrier rather than a company delivery fleet.

The proportion of variable costs in relation to sales varies widely according to the type of business. The variable costs of a discount retailer, the actual product costs, will be a large percentage of sales. For a ten-pin-bowling alley, the percentage of variable costs will be low. It would be wrong to assume, however, that a low proportion of variable costs will automatically create high profits and vice versa. The profit will be affected by the level of fixed costs within the business, regardless of the level of sales achieved.

Fixed costs

Fixed costs remain unchanged in the short term despite changes in sales volume, unless specific action is taken. These costs tend to be related to time rather than volume, such as monthly salaries and depreciation. Examples of fixed costs are:

- rent
- rates
- depreciation
- salaries
- cleaning costs

Clearly some costs are partly variable. An obvious example is the cost of telephones. There is a fixed charge and a variable charge. An important issue for a manufacturing company is the classification of production labour costs. These are directly connected with the cost of the product, but not necessarily variable. Few companies recruit and terminate production staff directly in relation to sales

Figure 1: Cash-flow forecast (six month example)

	Jan		Feb		March		April		May		June		Total	
	Projected	Actual	Projected	Actual	Projected	Actual	Projected	Actual	Projected	Actual	Projected	Actual	Projected	Actual
Receipts														
Sales – Cash														
Sales – Debtors														
Loans														
Other receipts														
A **Total receipts**														
Payments														
Cash purchases														
To creditors														
Wages and salaries (net)														
PAYE/NIC														
Capital items														
Rent/rates														
Services														
HP/leasing repayments														
Bank/finance charges														
Loan repayments														
Other payments:														
VAT (net)														
Corporation tax, etc.														
Dividend														
B **Total payments**														
Opening bank balance														
Add to B if overdrawn														
Subtract from B if credit														
C **Total**														
D **Closing bank balance (Difference between A&C)**														

volume. The likelihood is that the labour force is regarded as a fixed resource in the short term, and modest changes in sales volume are absorbed by changes in inventory levels.

For the sake of easy calculation, some companies identify the costs which are truly variable and classify the remainder as fixed. This is not entirely accurate, but is probably sufficient for the purpose.

Marginal profit

Marginal profit is defined as the sales revenue minus the variable cost of sales. An important figure to know for profit management is the percentage marginal profit:

Percentage of marginal profit =

$$\frac{\text{Sales revenue} - \text{variable cost of sales}}{\text{Sales revenue}} \times 100$$

If the sales of a company are £10.0m and the variable cost of sales is £5.5m, then the percentage marginal profit is:

Percentage of marginal profit

$$= \frac{£10m - £5.5m}{£10m}$$

$$= \frac{£4.5m}{£10m} = 45\%$$

It must not be assumed that a high percentage marginal profit will ensure high profits. An extreme example illustrates what may happen. Some years ago an electronics company formed a subsidiary company to make and sell silicon chips. It was realized at the outset that the

minimum viable size of production unit and the essential number of technical staff required would lead to substantial losses in the early years. During the third financial year, a 74 per cent marginal profit was achieved. As a result of actual sales still being much lower than the available capacity, however, the fixed costs were 205 per cent of sales revenue. So a loss of 131 per cent of sales resulted. In sharp contrast, the next year produced sales nearly three times higher and a modest profit was achieved.

Some managers assume that percentage marginal profit achieved by each product or service group will be virtually identical. In many businesses, the reality is dramatically different. For example, if the overall average marginal profit is 45 per cent, the figures for individual product or service groups may range from 30 to 60 per cent or even wider still.

Effective profit management requires maximizing not just the total sales value produced from a given level of fixed costs, but also the total amount of marginal profit which can be generated.

Unless the percentage of marginal profit is known for each product or service group, profit management is reduced to shooting in the dark. What is worse, customers have an uncannily accurate knack of recognizing bargain prices, even if the supplier is unaware that a bargain price is being offered, which means a best-selling product or service may result from the sales price reflecting a lower-than-average percentage marginal profit.

Ignorance of marginal profit percentages can be disastrous. A computer component manufacturer suffered a fall in selling prices from $2.25 to $0.79 in less than 18 months, because of overcapacity among suppliers. A once profitable company rapidly produced heavy losses. A policy decision was taken to capture more market share to eliminate the losses. Unfortunately the losses increased further. A company doctor was called in to save the business. It was rapidly established that the variable cost was $0.89, 10 cents higher than the selling price, with little scope for improvement using the existing facilities. The company had been leapfrogged by competitors using the latest technology to reduce costs substantially.

A knowledge of the percentage marginal profit produced by each product or service group enables the manager to increase profit by:

- ensuring that marketing effort is biased towards the products and services producing above average percentage marginal profit
- directing sales resources towards the above average percentage-marginal-profit lines. If appropriate, differential sales commission incentives should be introduced
- value engineering below-average products and services to increase the percentage marginal profit by reducing the variable cost where possible; and incorporating features which will command a disproportionately higher sales price as well
- making sure that any new products and services introduced will at least maintain the overall average marginal profit achieved by the business.

Other ingredients of effective profit management are:

- a knowledge of the break-even point of the business
- the management of product profitability
- the profitability achieved from key customers
- the dangers of marginal pricing.

Each of these aspects will now be described.

Break-even point

The break-even point of a business is the level of sales at which neither a profit nor a loss results.

A knowledge of the total fixed costs and the overall percentage marginal profit allows the break-even point to be calculated:

$$\text{Break-even point} = \frac{\text{Fixed costs}}{\substack{\text{Percentage} \\ \text{marginal profit}}}$$

The higher the percentage marginal profit, the greater is the impact of a change in sales volume on the profit before tax, and vice versa.

Product and service profitability

The calculation of the profit or loss before tax achieved by a product or service group involves guesswork in many businesses. The reason is that many of the staff and facilities in a complex business are shared by more than one product or service group. This means that accountants apportion or allocate a fair share of the common costs to individual products or services. Words such as 'apportion' and 'allocate' give a feel of scientific accuracy when a degree of informed guesswork is really what is involved. As a result, the profit or loss before tax calculated for a product or service group may be significantly inaccurate. This can lead to decisions to discontinue sales of a product on the basis of allocated as well as specific costs. If there is then nowhere else for the allocated costs to go, the overall profit will be reduced.

Customer profitability

Customer concentration is growing. Many businesses have one or more customers each of which account for at least 5 per cent of total invoiced sales. Quite often these customers are more demanding than less important ones. In addition to receiving lower prices or being given quantity discounts, other costs may be incurred as well.

Whenever a customer accounts for more than 5 per cent of total sales, the percentage marginal profit for the customer should be calculated. Also, if any additional overhead costs are incurred for a particular customer, these should be identified as well.

Marginal-pricing danger

This section has concentrated upon the importance of marginal-profit analysis to optimize customer, product and service profitability. Marginal pricing, in contrast, may well undermine existing profitability instead of improving it.

If there is spare capacity in a business, regardless of whether it is a manufacturer or a service company, one could argue that marginal pricing should be adopted. In other words, the surplus capacity should be sold at cut prices as long as some marginal profit is gained from each sale.

Arithmetically this appears attractive, but the real dangers are:

● the cut-price work undermines the normal priced business, or even substitutes for some of it
● a price war with competitors may be sparked off and prices generally may be reduced.

If it does make sense to utilize spare capacity by accepting business with lower profitability, important aspects are to:

● limit the amount of cut-price business and the period during which it will be offered, otherwise it may be so attractive to customers that overall profitability will fall
● offer a more basic specification than normal, to justify and preserve the price differential
● direct the cut-price business towards a different type of customer or country, so that the base business is not undermined.

4. Financial analysis for decision-making

Few major business decisions are so clear-cut that financial analysis can be safely ignored, because the benefits are so overwhelming. Some managers leave the financial analysis completely to an accountant. As the financial analysis could make or break the decision to proceed, this is an abdication of responsibility rather than delegation of the calculation involved.

Equally, many managers are unfamiliar with the most effective techniques of financial analysis to assist decision-making. Words such as discounted pay-back periods, internal rates of return, net present values and sensitivity analysis seem proof enough that financial analysis for decision-making is beyond the grasp of managers. Such an assumption is entirely wrong.

Financial analysis for decision-making requires:

- a knowledge of which technique is appropriate
- forecast of future revenues, costs and cash flows
- an understanding of the answer produced by the computer or calculator.

Technique

There is wide acceptance that the appropriate financial analysis technique for decision-making is based upon cash flow and not profit. Decisions should be based upon:

- future cash flows
- incremental and differential cash flows
- company-wide cash flows.

Each of these terms is sufficiently important to require further explanation.

Only *future* cash flows should be taken into account when making a decision. Past and irretrievable cash flows should be ignored.

The amount spent to date, and the extent to which costs have exceeded budget, are irrelevant for decision purposes. Regardless of whether the project proceeds or not, development costs to date will have to be charged to the profit and loss account. The decision needs to be based upon whether or not a further outlay is justified by the cash-flow benefits to be gained from the current estimate of future sales.

Incremental and differential cash flow is simpler than it sounds. Cash flows which will continue whether or not the decision to proceed is made should be ignored and only differences taken into account.

Costs which exist already and will not increase should be ignored completely and no attempt should be made to apportion a share of these costs when doing the financial analysis for decision-making.

The *company-wide* impact on cash flow must be assessed, and not merely the effect upon the department initiating the project. It would be wrong, for example, for a division developing a new product to ignore the cash-flow implications on, for example, the warehousing and distribution division. Either a new warehouse or an extension to the existing one may be needed, involving a substantial cash outlay. This must be included in the project evaluation.

In a similar way, the requirement of additional working capital must not be overlooked. Quite often working capital is a significant part of the overall cash-flow investment in an expansion project.

Evaluation

The criteria most commonly used to evaluate the cash-flow projection for a proposed project are:

- pay-back period
- discounted pay-back period
- percentage internal rate of return

● net present value.

Each of these now will be explained.

Pay-back period

This method simply calculates the time required for the incremental cash outflow to be recouped. For example, consider a project as follows:

Initial cash outlay:	£40,000
Annual cash inflow:	
Year 1	£ 5,000
2	£10,000
3	£15,000
4	£20,000
5	£10,000

Then the pay-back period is 3.5 years, as it will be halfway through the fourth year before the cumulative cash inflow equals the initial cash outflow of £40,000.

There are two obvious shortcomings of using the pay-back period for decision-making:

● interest costs on the cash outflow are ignored
● no consideration is given to either the duration or amount of cash inflow after the pay-back period.

Discounted pay-back period

The discounted pay-back method in discounted cash-flow (DCF) analysis takes into account the interest costs on the cash outflow. So the discounted pay-back period is the time required to recoup the initial cash outflow, at an assumed rate of interest. No consideration of what happens afterwards is taken into account.

Some companies assume a standard rate of interest when using discounted pay-back periods, on the assumption that the current interest rate may be temporarily high or low and not typical of the likely average interest rate during the pay-back period. Also, by choosing a standard rate of interest, a maximum pay-back period can be set in order for a decision to proceed to be taken. In the previous example, the pay-back period was 3.5 years. If a standard interest rate of 10 per cent is assumed, the discounted pay-back period would be 4.3 years. Using a typical bank overdraft rate of, say 15 per cent, the discounted pay-back period would be in excess of 5 years.

Percentage internal rate of return (IRR)

This is often referred to as the percentage IRR (or as the DCF rate of return). If the cash flows from a project are calculated to give a 17 per cent IRR, after tax, this means that the weighted average return, taking into account the changes in the net cash outflow which are expected to occur during the project, and calculated net of corporation tax, over the assumed effective life of the project, is 17 per cent.

This allows a company to set a minimum percentage IRR for projects to be authorized. Many companies require a minimum percentage IRR of at least 15 per cent net of tax.

The effective life of the project is not necessarily the useful physical life of the assets. For example, some purpose-built electronic test equipment may perform satisfactorily for at least 20 years. The effective life of the project may be only five years, however, because by then the market demand for the particular product will have expired.

Net present value (NPV)

Net present value is another variation of discounted cash-flow techniques, but the most abstract one for managers to use. Generally speaking, the percentage IRR is much more widely used and easier to understand.

As some companies do use net present value, often abbreviated to NPV, it will be described briefly. The NPV is the net present value of all the cash outflows and inflows, discounted at a standard percentage rate chosen by the company. For example, the NPV of the cash flows in the previous example, discounted at 15 per cent, is net outflow of £1,280.

Such an answer seems to beg the question: is this an acceptable return or not? One method of answering this is to calculate a NPV Index, defined as:

NPV index =

$$\frac{\text{NPV, at assumed rate of return}}{\text{Maximum cash outflow}}$$

This still requires a second calculation, compared to the percentage IRR method.

Sensitivity analysis

Sensitivity analysis allows the impact of different possible outcomes to be evaluated easily. It is sometimes described as 'what if?' analysis, because it answers the question 'what if such and such were to happen?'

Typical outcomes which can be evaluated are:

- What if development work costs 5 per cent more than forecast?
- What if the sales launch is delayed by six months?
- What if sales in the first year are 10 per cent below forecast?
- What if sales prices are 1 per cent higher or lower than forecast?

The management role

The manager responsible for the project or investment must play a major part in the forecast of sales volumes, selling prices and operating costs from which the cash flows will be calculated. The accountant may well be better equipped than the manager to produce the cash-flow analysis, but must not be allowed to make assumptions about sales volumes, selling prices, staffing levels and operating costs. This is the area in which the manager must provide the requisite knowledge of the market-place and the method of operation.

Similarly, the manager should be better equipped than an accountant to know the key vulnerabilities which the project may encounter. So the manager should suggest specific 'what if?' calculations to be carried out. The accountant should carry out additional 'what if?' calculations to highlight other situations to which the rate of return would be particularly sensitive.

Equally, the manager must understand not only what the answer calculated by the accountant means but why the company requires a given maximum rate of return. Simply to achieve a rate of return comparable with current overdraft interest rates is totally unacceptable, for several reasons:

- managers tend to be optimistic when projecting the future cash flow to be achieved from an investment, so allowance has to be made in the rate of return required.

- occasionally, a project will fail substantially or be aborted after considerable expense has been involved
- in some businesses, about one-fifth of total investment does not generate a cash flow in return, because it is required for essential replacement, refurbishment or to meet legislation
- and not least, there should be some return achieved for the benefit of shareholders to reward them for the commercial risk involved.

So it is not surprising that many companies require a rate of return of at least 25 per cent a year, before the effect of corporation tax is taken into account.

Investment risks and rewards

Many companies set one required rate of return for all investment situations regardless of the differing risks and uncertainties involved. This has the merit of simplicity. It could result, however, in decisions to:

- reject projects such as an investment to reduce existing costs, where there is a minimum of risk and uncertainty, because the return falls a bit short of the required minimum
- approve projects which are speculative, such as an investment to launch a new product in an overseas market.

Merchant bankers and financial institutions recognize the need for an acceptable balance between potential risk and reward. Different rates of return are required on investment in management buy-outs compared with venture-capital finance for newly formed companies.

A small proportion of large companies adopt a similar approach by setting different rates of return according to the degree of risk involved in various categories of projects. Possible categories are:

- improved efficiency on existing business, e.g. investment in automation, mechanical handling, improved test facilities
- expansion of existing products or services in existing markets and countries
- diversification into either a new product or service in an existing market or country, or vice versa
- a new product or service in a new market or country.

Clearly, the rate of return required should increase in each of the above categories. To set differential rates of return requires considerable expertise. None the less, there is a case for adopting a somewhat flexible approach, even if somewhat subjectively, to investment decision-making. Low-risk projects perhaps should be approved even if the required return is not quite demonstrated. In contrast, an investment which involves considerable diversification and only just achieves the necessary return, requires the utmost scrutiny.

Application

The cash-flow analysis techniques described in this chapter are widely applicable. They can be used to evaluate:

- *Lease versus buy decisions.* The cost of outright purchase and the regular lease payments can be compared to calculate the percentage IRR (internal rate of return), which is the effective percentage annual cost of leasing.

- *Make versus buy decisions*. The differential cash flows of making in-house compared with buying the product or service are used to calculate the percentage IRR.
- *Expansion projects*. The cash outflow required to finance capital expenditure and working capital is compared with the incremental cash inflow produced throughout the assumed project life to calculate the percentage IRR.
- *Company acquisitions*. The cost of acquisition is compared with the total incremental cash-flow benefit to the acquirer to calculate a percentage IRR.

Commercial factors

It must never be forgotten that an acceptable rate-of-return calculation is not sufficient to justify an investment decision. In addition, the proposed investment needs to be:

- consistent with the chosen corporate strategy and commercial rationale of the business
- the most suitable method to achieve the required goal, after consideration of the different alternatives available
- an acceptable balance between potential reward and interest risk
- acceptable to customers, suppliers and staff, where appropriate.

Project Management

7.1 Introduction

Project management is a core management technique widely applicable to most business activities from planning a company meeting or launching a new product to building a major engineering works or introducing a large computer installation.

A project can be looked upon as an undertaking that has a set of activities that are linked together over a period of time to achieve an established goal or goals. Project management is concerned with the management of these activities to ensure that the goals are attained to the right *quality*, on *time* and within *budget*.

A project has three chief attributes:

(1) a clearly defined objective
(2) infrequent, unique or unfamiliar to the enterprise undertaking its execution
(3) complex, often having an intricate physical performance and time structure.

All projects therefore have a definite life-span and may therefore be said to come and go within an organization that has a continuing existence. Furthermore projects draw upon the existing resources on a part-time basis which often leads to conflict with departmental heads. Essentially good project management demands the efficient juggling of limited resources in a set time-frame to achieve a desired goal.

Today society's needs are increasing in scale. As jobs become more demanding they tend to become less like any other job previously undertaken. A new kind of organization and new ways of running these jobs are needed. Particular problems arise because the project organization is accommodated within the existing group of service skills which are to be found in conventional structures.

Consequently project managers have to exercise control over expenditure, the use of special skills and a programme while the company as a whole is free to engage in other activities.

7.2 Project life cycle

It is helpful when discussing the planning and control of any project to consider the project life cycle. The life cycle concept can be applied to any type of project such as: the introduction of a new product, a large power station, a communication or transportation system, or the publication of a book. Any system or product, whether hardware, software, biological or economic is dynamic and goes through a number of distinct stages. It is created, developed, grows to maturity and then declines and is phased out.

As a project proceeds through this life cycle certain essential events or milestones of achievement are reached. These can be represented as indicated in Figure 2, and form manageable 'chunks' of work which may be broken down into well-defined

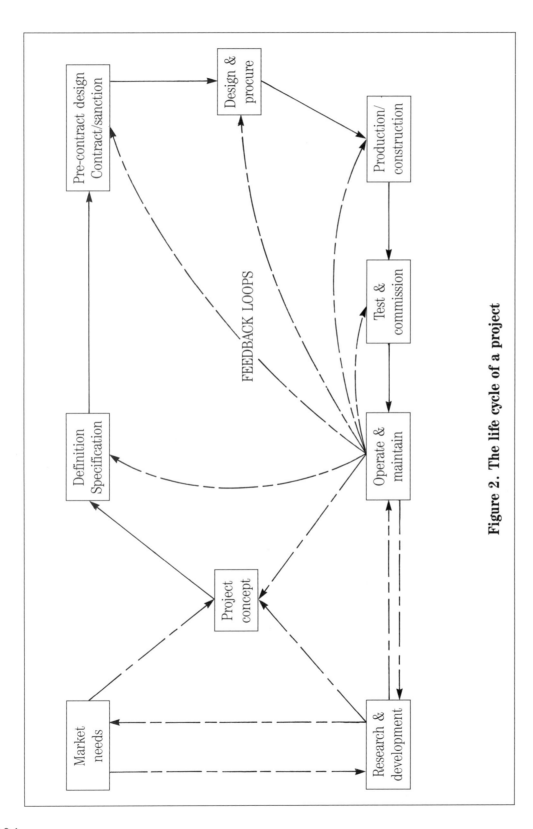

Figure 2. The life cycle of a project

Statements of Work (SOW).

Management is concerned with planning the defined work and obtaining action on the agreed plan as well as monitoring and applying control to achieve the desired results.

1. Defining the project

It is important at the outset to evaluate the economic consequences of undertaking a project. The project must be assessed in the light of the company's strategic guidelines. While it is important to 'do things right' it is even more important to 'do right things'. Many project selection procedures are available but are outside the scope of this book. Sufficient to say that before embarking on any project a clear understanding of its aims, viability and 'fit' within the corporate plan must be assessed.

Once a project has been selected it is useful to write down both the technical and commercial objectives. This provides focus for the planning and helps to steer the project through to its conclusion. Defining project objectives may require substantial effort and research. A STEP (social, technical, economical and political) analysis may aid definition. Market research is crucial to enable meaningful objectives to be set.

Global objectives such as increasing performance or making more profit are too broad to be of any use. Objectives should be specific and quantifiable. By setting 'how much' and 'when' targets the project can be more focused. If accurate objectives cannot be set at the outset of the project, best guess values must be inserted and then firmed up or revised as the project evolves.

While project management has as its main goal the satisfying of a specified performance within an agreed time-scale and budget these are really undesirable constraints within which the work has to be conducted. They are not the real objectives of the project which could be:

- to capture a larger share of a market
- to prepare for future development
- to utilize surplus by-products, and so on.

Therefore positive steps must be taken to explain the aim of the project to all concerned. Good communication is the essence of management in project work where team leadership becomes vital. Such measures may range from briefing sessions taking an hour or two, to residential courses.

Work commences at the procurement specification stage, where the basic needs are ascertained and it becomes necessary to produce performance, time and cost documents, describing possible ways of meeting the specifications. This initial work may be in the form of tender or feasibility studies. Such studies will be for the complete project and will include details such as weight, power, quality, reliability, maintainability, and so on, as well as the linking factors of time and cost. The total progression of a project is from the initial feasibility study through to the project definitions, design, development, production and actual operation. It is the job of a project manager to steer, co-ordinate and drive a project throughout all the phases of activity within the enterprise for which he works. In a sense the project manager acts as the mediator between the customer and the company. Once a contract has been accepted his whole attention is directed towards achieving the technical performance, delivery time and cost estimates agreed with the customer. Thus a project manager is held responsible for the execution of a contract to the customer's satisfaction. Essentially he deals with the *what*, *when*, and *where* aspects but not with the *how* of the project. This does not mean however that he is never concerned with the *how* aspects. Indeed he may have to step in to spot any false work being undertaken.

2. The specification

A specification is a description in precise terms. In project work documents within this common title serve many, very different, purposes. An appreciation of what makes a good specification in one circumstance is not necessarily helpful in writing for another.

There are some qualities to be found in all these documents; the emphasis and relevance varies with the purpose.

(1) Qualities

Among the qualities important in a specification are completeness, relevance, unambiguousness, adequacy and consistency. It also needs to be user friendly.

Completeness

The single feature which most people agree is essential to a specification is that it should be specific. As far as possible nothing important should be left to the discretion of the reader. The greatest practical difficulty is in matching all the details of the entity with statements. At the beginning of a project this is usually owing to lack of imagination or communication; in the middle, the sheer mass of detail and the task of effecting correspondence.

Relevance

It is useless to specify anything which is not to be commanded or which is already available in a rather different but standard form. It not infrequently happens that A contracts with B to create an item whose function is already well served by an item known to neither of them. One of the best contributions the computer can make to design is to prevent wasting resources on redundant activity by retrieving information.

Unambiguousness

The customer may not be entirely certain what he wants. If so the submission of a specification to a customer is the wrong occasion for clarifying his ideas, unless it is not yet the basis of the contract. Relations between project manager and designer are sometimes marred by the former saying, in effect, 'I cannot tell you what I want but I will know it when I see it'.

Adequacy

Unless the specification is only sufficient to meet the *true* needs of the circumstances the relationship between cost and performance may never be properly established.

Consistency

A specification includes several separate requirements which are to be satisfied simultaneously. This is only possible if they are not mutually exclusive.

(2) The forms of specifications

In order to regulate the decision-making at each stage of a project it is important to determine the form of the specifications.

Many organizations have elaborate rules for the preparation of drawings, but it is less common to find adequate guidelines for writing the antecedent documents. To be effective they should be closely adapted to the local requirements.

7.3 Project programmes and the organization

No project can succeed if there is an inadequate strategy for tackling the basic problems. A programme is a statement of intention setting out the milestones of achievement towards clearly defined objectives. From the previous definitions it will be clear that any such statements of intent have a large element of uncertainty written into them, since what is to be tackled has probably never been attempted before, either on such a scale, or in such a manner. Project management therefore is concerned with the management of activities to ensure that the goals are achieved to the right standard, on time and within budget and therefore is concerned with *planning*, *controlling*, and *organizing*.

1. The programme

The programme specifies what work has to be undertaken and therefore defines the scope of the project and acts as a yardstick against which performance achievement can be monitored for control purposes. Because of uncertainty the initial pro-

gramme for any project may well have to be altered as a project proceeds, but the criterion of a good programme lies in the ability it allows for adaption to crises as they occur. The dimensions of any programme will be in terms of resources required, and time and cost allocation. The project manager will be responsible for laying down the programme to be achieved, and for this purpose he will have to consult with the task performers in all phases of the contract. As a task setter he may often require specialist project engineers to make up part of his own team.

Programme objectives can be broken down into a series of tasks with definite achievement goals. These are generally called *activities* and *events*, activities represent time, and events represent finite achievements and, therefore, have no time duration. The development of PERT (programme evaluation review techniques) and CPM (critical path method), did, in fact, originate out of large-scale, complex technical projects.

It is the essence of such techniques that the activities and events are fitted together to form a network which represents the complete logical structure of the project as a whole. Such an overall display then allows those responsible for the various activities to estimate durations and resources, be they material or human, that are needed. This information enables the project manager to predict completion dates of the project and/or parts of it, and so ascertain how interactions between his programme and other concurrent programmes will be managed. It is vitally important for a project manager to break down a project into activities that can be identified and tackled by individuals or particular departments or subcontractors. By this means he establishes a sound, proper operational relationship with the specialist group skills.

2. The work-package structure

The complementary roles of the project manager and the functional manager centre around the work to be accomplished – the work package. A work package is an integral sub-element of the project; a sub-system; a sub-product, etc. A work breakdown structure for any project can be represented by a pyramid similar to that used for describing traditional organizational structures. Such a structure can be broken down by portions of hardware and then by functions associated with each aspect of the work. A typical work breakdown structure is indicated in Figure 3.

The work breakdown analysis and the resulting work packages provide a model of the products (hardware, software, services and other outputs) that completely define the project. Such a model enables project engineers, project managers, functional managers, and general managers to think of the totality of all items and services necessary for completing the project. The work breakdown structure with accompanying work packages is necessary to accomplish the required actions for managing a project as it:

- summarizes all products and services comprised in the project, including support and other tasks
- displays the inter-relationships of the work packages to each other, to the total project, and to other engineering activities in the organization
- establishes the authority–responsibility matrix organization
- enables the estimate of project cost to be obtained
- ensures correct scheduling of work packages
- develops information for managing the project
- provides a basis for controlling the application of resources on the project and a reference point for getting people committed to support the project.

7.4 Planning and the project life cycle

All projects need a plan, but planning without action is futile and action without planning is fatal. The plan clearly defines what is to be done, why and by whom, when and for how much. The plan outlines the strategy of how future events are to be undertaken. It becomes the standard for control but unlike physical

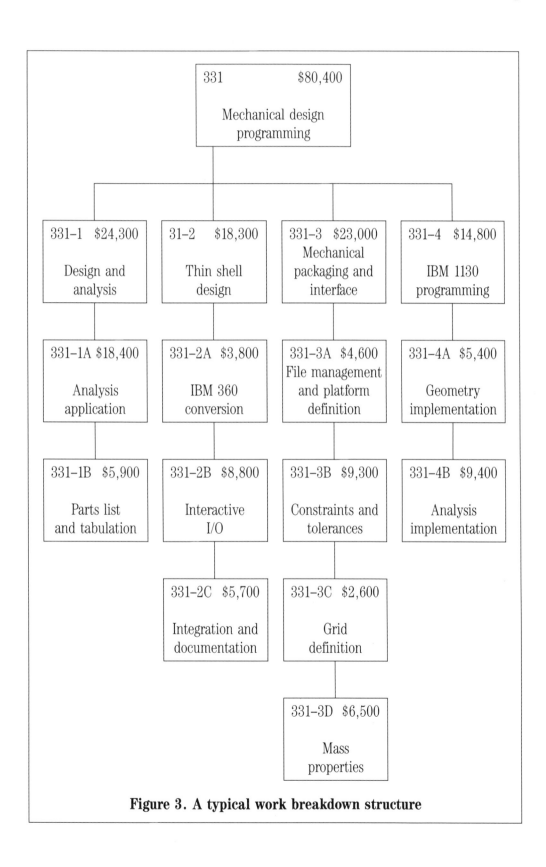

Figure 3. A typical work breakdown structure

standards it is often changing in the light of performance. The project manager has constantly to adjust the plan to combat disturbances and regulate action.

Throughout the project's life cycle the plan becomes a key communication document for the co-ordination of the various work packages that have to be undertaken.

Essential elements of a project plan

No matter what size of project is being undertaken the essential elements of a project plan are:

(1) A summary of the essentials of the project written in such a manner that anyone can get a grasp of all that is entailed. It states briefly what is to be done and how it is to be done, and lists the end-product or service.
(2) A work breakdown structure that has enough detail to identify the relationships of work packages, work units and job numbers.
(3) A citation of tangible key milestones that can be counted, measured, and evaluated in such a way that there can be no ambiguity as to whether or not a milestone has been achieved. There should be a correspondence of milestones to project budgets to facilitate adequate monitoring.
(4) An event logic network that shows the

sequencing of the elements (work packages) of the project and how they are to be related – which can be done in parallel, series, etc. Such a network may be turned into bar charts for easy reading.
(5) An organization interface plan that shows how the project relates with the rest of the world – customer, line-staff organizations, sub-contractors, suppliers, and other clientele that have some role in the project.
(6) A reporting plan for how the project is to be reviewed – who reviews the project, when, and for what purpose.
(7) A list of key project personnel and their assignments in the project.

While the project plan need not be elaborate for a small project there still has to be a plan which should be depicted in the simplest possible way. The danger with large projects is that the plan often gets too big too soon. Control then becomes difficult to exercise.

When the plan has been formulated, a programme of work can be produced as a set of time schedules so that the *When* and the *How much* of each work package can be determined. Separate budgets and schedules may be drawn up for every project element and given to the individuals who are to be held responsible for them.

7.5 Progressing the agreed plan

Any project programme requires analysis, expresses policy and should lead to control. The programme must be depicted so that it strikes a balance between the necessity for including essential infor-

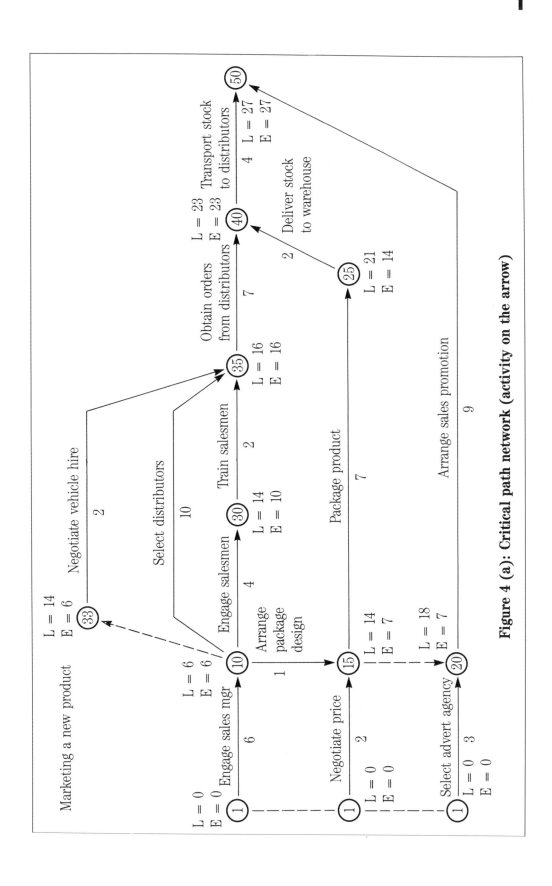

Figure 4 (a): Critical path network (activity on the arrow)

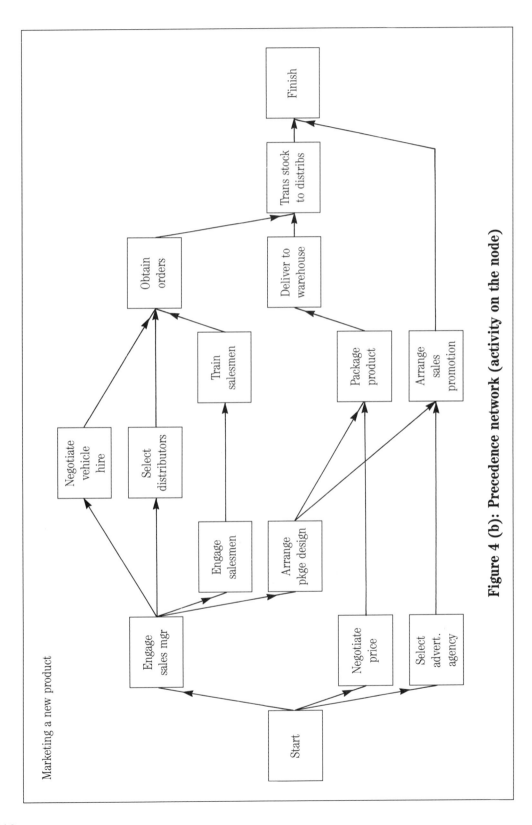

Marketing a new product

Figure 4 (b): Precedence network (activity on the node)

mation and the requirements of simplicity. If the chart is too complicated it loses its value because it cannot be readily understood; if it is not easy to read regular progressing of the project tends to lapse and the chart falls into disuse.

There are several forms of presentation which can be used:

1. Network analysis

Network analysis is a method of preparing programmes in such a way that they can be analysed to identify both the critical and non-critical activities and their inter-relationships. A network diagram is a generic title for programmes produced by this method. Examples of such diagrams are:

● the critical path diagram (sometimes known as the activity-on-the arrow diagram), see Figure 4(a).
● the precedence diagram (alternatively known as the activity-on-the-node diagram), see Figure 4(b).

Such diagrams are prepared to determine the logical sequence, inter-relationships and timing of the activities and the shortest time in which the programme can be completed. However, apart from a well-drawn linked bar chart, such diagrams are usually large, complicated and obscure to all but the drafter and other planning engineers. Inevitably they are poor media for communication with, and interpretation by, the people who are going to use them. In general it is better to break the networks down to small 'fragments' which are then depicted as bar charts.

Basically a network diagram is a programming tool. It only becomes a control tool if it is regularly monitored and updated. In the past programmes in the form of critical path or precedence diagrams have fallen into disrepute not necessarily because of any lack of accuracy in initial programming logic but through management's failure regularly to update the programme to reflect actual progress.

The most effective method of monitoring such a network programme and measuring the effects of delay is to ensure that the programme is continuously updated after each progress review, preferably by computer – firstly with a time analysis to assess current progress in relation to the completion date and secondly, where there is a projected overrun and it is not possible to extend the end date, a revised resource-analysis re-scheduled with the additional resources and programmed to maintain the existing completion date.

Such monitoring is however relatively expensive, requires the continuous attention of a programmer, the commitment and full understanding of the programme team and, if possible, the availability of a computer to provide a programme update after each progress review. Furthermore, even on some of those projects where regular updating is carried out, neither the contractor's team nor the project design team have the resources to make full and effective use of the programme review data.

In practice either the updating is not carried out and the programme rapidly becomes out of date or the updating is carried out but the implications are not fully understood and the appropriate action is not taken as it should be. In either case the programme loses credibility as a

Figure 5: Schedule with cost and manpower

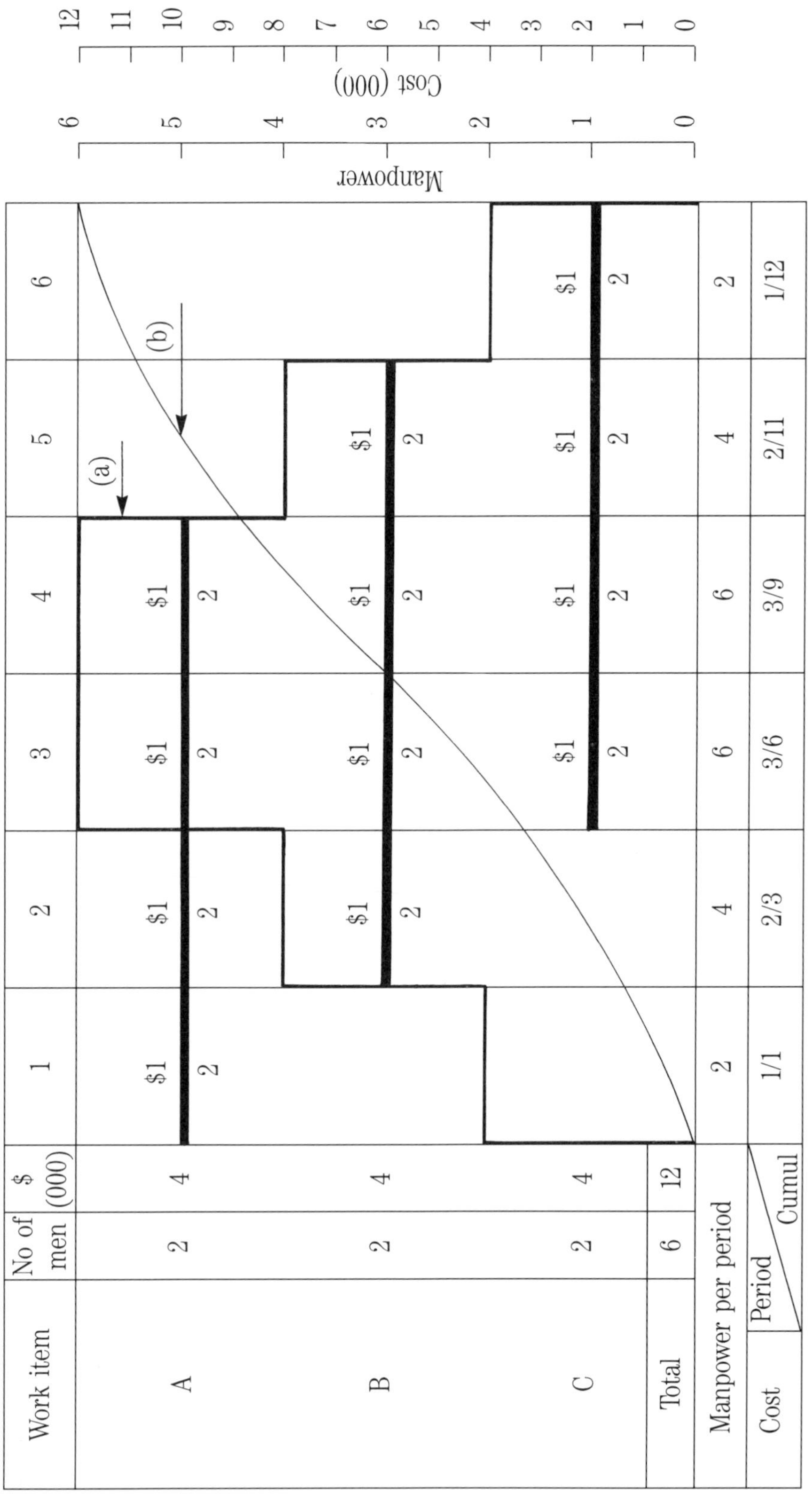

Period of time

Work item	No of men	$ (000)	1	2	3	4	5	6
A	2	4	$1 2	$1 2	$1 2	$1 2 (a)		
B	2	4		$1 2	$1 2	$1 2	$1 2	
C	2	4			$1 2	$1 2	$1 2	$1 2 (b)
Total	6	12						
Manpower per period			2	4	6	6	4	2
Cost	Period / Cumul		1/1	2/3	3/6	3/9	2/11	1/12

Manpower

6	5	4	3	2	1	0

Cost (000)

12	11	10	9	8	7	6	5	4	3	2	1	0

control tool and is left on the wall to fade away in the course of time while the team get on with the job with the aid of 'meaningful' bar charts.

A critical path or precedence diagram, despite its value as a programming tool to work out the duration and sequence of operation and the timing of a project, may need to be redrawn in bar chart form, preferably as a linked bar chart, in such a way as to continue to show the inter-relationship and timing of the activities and the critical path.

2. Bar charts

Activites are set against a time-scale so the plan and the schedule are shown together. See Figure 5, here three activity types A, B and C are represented on a time-scale. This figure can also be used to depict the manpower requirements and the cost of each activity. The manpower can be aggregated up to give a histogram of the manpower loading as in Figure 5 at (a) and a complete cost curve as at (b).

7.6 Controlling the programme

Control is really the counterpart of the programme and work statements. Planning sets the goals to be obtained and looks forward. Control combats disturbances and regulates action en route to the goals, and looks backwards to check the correct path has been followed.

Any control system requires measure-ments to be taken and comparison against set standards and finally appropriate action. Control is exercised by measuring *time*, *cost*, *resources* and *performance* and like the control of any physical system operates on a closed loop feedback system (see Figure 6).

Controls should be future shaping devices. They must operate according to the views of what tomorrow can and should bring forth. A manager does not want overshoot or undershoot of his goals, for this will mean waste of time, money, material and effort. Control has to be

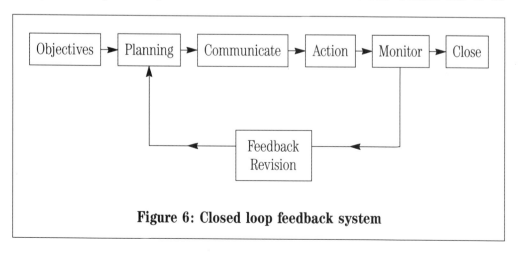

Figure 6: Closed loop feedback system

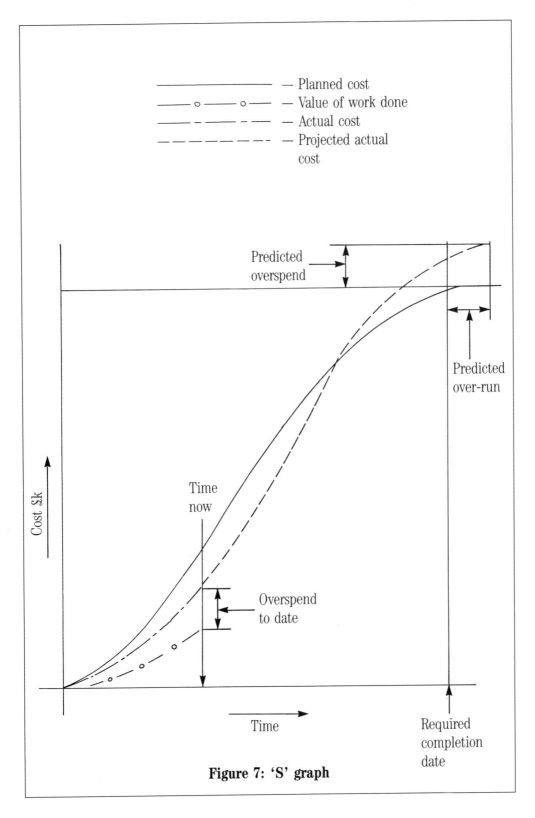

Figure 7: 'S' graph

applied to cost, time and material resources and to performance.

1. Presenting the standard

As mentioned previously it is necessary to present plans pictorially so that the standard to be achieved at any instant can be recognized and any deviation determined. There are many useful programme charts which can be used, from histograms, pie charts, slip graphs and the socalled 'S' type graphs.

To illustrate the project control process only the 'S' type graph will be used and control of cost considered (see Figure 7).

2. Using the 'S' graph as means of control

The control of cost implies that there are costs which are controllable and that merit consideration. Obviously it would be uneconomical to spend £1.50 to control costs of £1.00.

Any task can be cost estimated by breaking the task down into conventional statements of work (SOW), and each statement cost can be added together to give an overall budget cost which may be allocated to the relevant accountancy periods.

In order to control costs it is necessary to collect all costs incurred at each review time. It must be appreciated that *actual* costs are those which have passed through the company's books whereas *committed* costs represent firm orders whose costs have not yet been invoiced. Also at each review point estimates of the cost to completion of work started but not yet completed can be given. By adding these amounts together a new estimate of the total cost of the overall engineering task can be obtained.

Figure 7 shows a typical 'S' type budget planned cost curve for a project. The current position at the review 'Time now' is obtained by deriving the cost value of the work done and comparing it with the budgeted expenditure and the actual costs incurred.

In this example, although *actual* does not exceed *planned* – at this time – it does significantly exceed *value*. This means that, while the project is not exceeding the planned rate of spend, it is also not achieving the progress expected for the costs so far incurred.

By taking a series of reviews, and making similar comparisons the true position of the project with regard to cost and time of completion can be ascertained and an estimate of predicted overspend and over-run given (see Figure 7). The frequency of the review times will depend on the accuracy of control required and the cost of obtaining the information. The project manager must make this decision and ensure that any necessary action is implemented if wide variations occur.

For any project the art of control by the project manager is to regulate the pace of working so that the desired client objective is achieved. In doing this the project manager may exercise his prerogative by suggesting trade offs between time, cost and performance.

7.7 Final handover to the client

The final phase of any project concerns handing over to the essential users. Where hardware is concerned this will often necessitate commissioning the equipment to ensure that all items are working satisfactorily and performing in accordance with the specification. This requires the planning of a testing programme and the sign off of the various test results – may be to the satisfaction of some approved authority.

7.8 Main characteristics of project managers

The project manager is guardian of the time-scale and custodian of project experience. It is, therefore, imperative that any would-be project manager should be able to see ahead: he cannot afford to dabble in technical details, but needs to be able to programme those who do. That is not to imply that he never gets involved in technical detail, indeed, he may well have to on certain occasions when a trade-off situation arises. He should be hardware-orientated and keen to see ideas turned into working solutions. He will consequently need to have some technical and commercial knowledge. In addition, the lessons learned from any project should be recorded, together with the project history, so that information is readily available in a relevant form for future work. This sweeping up operation may well require a different type of person from those who started the project. For this reason some organizations have found it useful to appoint different project managers as the project progresses: a kind of rotating leadership.

Case histories have shown that successful project managers have come from various disciplines and departments in enterprises, from commercial departments to post development services. Looking at a variety of project managers the main common characteristics appear to be:

- strong, forceful but acceptable personality – diplomacy and advocacy should be strong traits
- intelligence with independence of mind
- proven ability in at least one branch of work essential to the project
- an appreciation of areas of work outside his experience and the ability to see things in the whole
- a vital interest and concern to see a project completed
- an ability to direct and delegate technical work
- business acumen – financial procedures, contract law, etc. – and entrepreneurial dynamism
- energy and resourcefulness.

7.9 Support for project management

Finally for projects to be successfully executed not only must there be good planning and control and an appropriate organizational structure but adequate top management support for project managers. Briefly, such support amounts to:

- clearly defined decision channels
- action on request
- assistance in conflict resolution

- resource provision, when needed
- long-range information
- advice and stage-setting support
- protection from political in-fighting
- opportunity for personal and professional growth.

Equally top management will expect from project managers the following:

- results and accountability
- effective reports and information
- minimum organizational disruption
- capacity to handle people problems
- self-starting capacity
- growth with the assignment.

Human Resources Management

8.1 The People Factor

'People are our most important asset' is a time honoured cliché and no chief executive or senior manager would disagree with the essential truth of it. Yet the reality for many organizations is that their people continue to remain under-valued, under-trained and under-utilized.

For organizations to survive and prosper in the 1990s a more radical and fundamental approach to people management will need to be considered. The impact of accelerating technological change together with increased economic, regulatory, social and demographic change demands organizations that are flexible and responsive. The rate of change has never been greater and organizations must absorb and manage change at a much faster rate than ever before.

A recent survey of chief executives revealed that two of the most significant problems in trying to implement a business strategy were:

(1) not having the right people capable of delivering the strategy
(2) a failure to train people effectively.

As access to the latest manufacturing processes, financial software controls and information technology becomes widely available, one of the few areas left that offers real sustainable competitive advantage is people. While information technology will continue to render enormous competitive advantages, the need to manage the people and the technology interface will become critical to realizing the full benefits of investment in it. Senior managers might consider how much existing IT capability is unrealized in their organization because people have not been properly trained to exploit it.

At the same time technology will continue to redefine and reshape industrial boundaries and skill levels. Most organizations experienced the impact of new technology in the 1980s but there is now a realization that technologies are converging. This raises fundamental skill and resourcing issues. For example, the distinctions between the computer and telecommunications industries are becoming increasingly blurred.

Customer service functions are being reorganized to take account of intelligent machine and systems diagnostics which replace the need for expensive service engineers. Many customer repair faults can now be repaired over a normal telephone line. The emphasis is switching from people with technical skills to those who swap printed circuit boards and display high levels of customer care.

At the other end of the scale the situation is being reversed, with technology creating a technocratic elite people who are highly trained, mobile, scarce and much sought after. The result is a polarization of skill levels within the organization.

The search for highly prized 'silver collared' knowledge workers will become an increasing problem for organizations. All businesses will be trying to ensure that they get their fair quota of talented staff. This will increase pressure for more innovative pay and reward schemes as well as a more sophisticated approach to career development. People management will become a strategic issue. No longer will organizations be able to simply rely upon pay as the main weapon in recruitment. Knowledge workers demand more. Organizations will need to offer a total career development package of which pay is just an element. Training and career development opportunities will become major items on the knowledge workers shopping list (see Figure 8).

Technology is also forcing senior managers to review their organization structures and consider the traditional role of the middle manager. In the past the middle manager was a conduit, filtering and passing information from the top to the bottom of the organization. On-line computer systems and information networks make this role redundant. The question then becomes what do we do with our middle managers? Demographic issues may mean that organizations will have to embrace the concept of retraining and re-educating rather than lose knowledgeable staff.

Changing social values and environmental concerns are also having an impact on people's views towards work, management development and career planning.

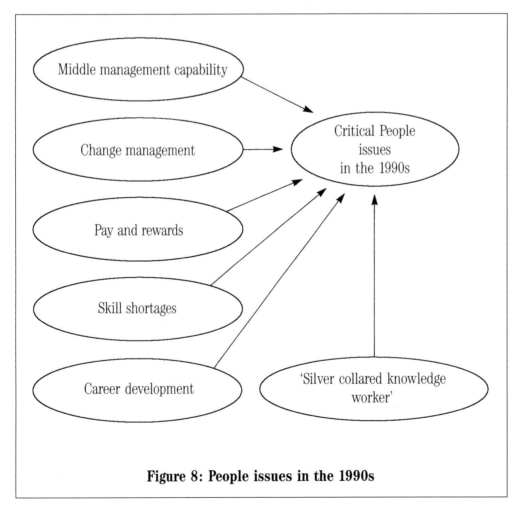

Figure 8: People issues in the 1990s

Changes in this area are likely to generate increasing organizational concern. Research is emerging which indicates that the aspirations and values of our management tier are changing. Stanford Research International (SRI) in the United States has identified a new breed of manager who seeks a career that mirrors his own personal values rather than those of the organization. The London Business School has recently conducted research into middle-management values and aspirations, and has identified serious dissatisfaction with existing organization life and the pressures being exerted on middle managers. Its conclusions pose major questions for future career development and planning activities. Many managers it appears are becoming increasingly tired of being asked to do 'more with less'. The attraction of working for large businesses is losing its appeal. Many managers are seeking greater independence and autonomy away from the pressures and stress of corporate life.

At the same time environmental issues and concerns are forcing organizations to reconsider their methods and operations.

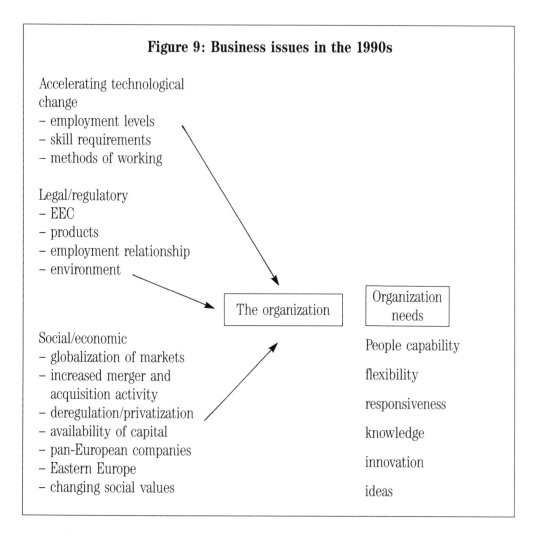

Figure 9: Business issues in the 1990s

Accelerating technological change
– employment levels
– skill requirements
– methods of working

Legal/regulatory
– EEC
– products
– employment relationship
– environment

Social/economic
– globalization of markets
– increased merger and acquisition activity
– deregulation/privatization
– availability of capital
– pan-European companies
– Eastern Europe
– changing social values

The organization

Organization needs

People capability

flexibility

responsiveness

knowledge

innovation

ideas

So called 'dirty businesses' whose products or services are viewed as damaging to the environment are having to deal with the fact that some people will no longer be attracted to work for them (see Figure 9).

8.2 Human Resource (HR) Strategy

Faced with such rapid change organizations need to develop a more focused and coherent approach to managing people. In just the same way a business requires a marketing or information technology strategy it also requires a human resource or people strategy. In developing such a strategy two critical questions must be addressed.

- What kinds of people do you need to manage and run your business to meet your strategic business objectives?
- What people programmes and initiatives must be designed and implemented to attract, develop and retain staff to compete effectively?

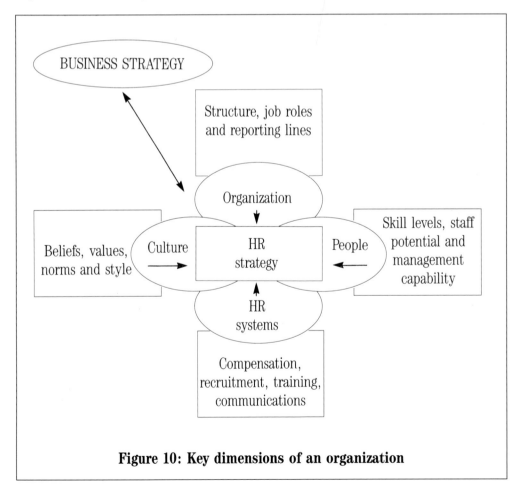

Figure 10: Key dimensions of an organization

In order to answer these questions four key dimensions of an organization must be addressed (see Figure 10). These are:

(1) Culture –
the beliefs, values, norms and management style of the organization

(2) Organization –
the structure, job roles and reporting lines of the organization

(3) People –
the skill levels, staff potential and management capability

(4) Human resources systems –
the people focused mechanisms which deliver the strategy – communications, training, rewards, career development, etc.

Frequently in managing the people element of their business senior managers will only focus on one or two dimensions and neglect to deal with the others. Typically companies reorganize their structures to free managers from bureaucracy and drive for more entrepreneurial flair but then fail to adjust their training or reward systems. When the desired entrepreneurial behaviour does not emerge managers frequently look confused at the apparent failure of the changes to deliver results. The fact is that seldom can you focus on only one area. What is required is a strategic perspective aimed at identifying the relationship between all four dimensions.

If you require an organization which really values quality and service you not only have to retrain staff, you must also review the organization, reward, appraisal and communications systems. The pay and reward system is a classic problem in this area. Frequently organizations have payment systems which are designed around the volume of output produced. If you then seek to develop a company which emphasizes the product's quality you must change the pay systems. Otherwise you have a contradiction between what the chief executive is saying about quality and what your payment system is encouraging staff to do.

There are seven steps to developing a *human resource strategy* and the active involvement of senior line managers should be sought throughout the approach (see Figure 11).

Step 1

- Understand your business strategy.
- Highlight the key driving forces of your business. What are they? e.g. technology, distribution.
- What are the implications of the driving forces for the people side of your business? What is the fundamental people contribution to bottom line business performance?

Step 2

- Develop a Mission Statement or Statement of Intent relating to the people side of the business.
- Do not be put off by negative reactions to the words or references to idealistic statements – it is the actual process of thinking through the issues in a formal and explicit manner that is important. What do your people contribute?

Figure 11: Developing a human resources strategy: explicit link between business and human resources strategy

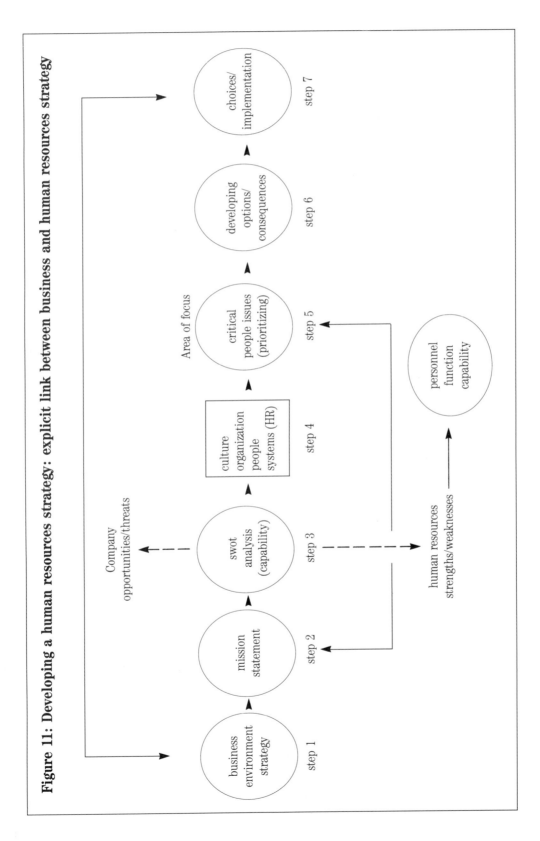

Step 3

- Conduct a SWOT (strengths, weak-nesses, opportunities and threats) analysis of the organization.
- Focus on the internal strengths and weaknesses of the people side of the business. Consider the current skill and capability issues.
- Vigorously research the external busi-ness and market environment. High-light the opportunities and threats relating to the people side of the business. What impact will/might they have on business performance? Con-sider skill shortages? The impact of new technology on staffing levels?
- From this analysis you then need to review the capability of your personnel department. Complete a SWOT analysis of the department – consider in detail the department's current areas of operation, the service levels and competences of your personnel staff.

Step 4

- Conduct a detailed human resources (HR) analysis, concentrate on the organization's culture, organization, people and HR systems (COPS)
- Consider: Where you are now? Where you want to be?
- What gaps exists between the reality of where you are now and where you want to be?
- You must exhaust your analysis of the four dimensions.

Step 5

- Go back to the business strategy and

examine it against your SWOT and COPS Analysis.
- Identify the critical people issues – namely those people issues that you *must* address. Those which have a key impact on the delivery of your business strategy.
- Prioritize the critical people issues. What will happen if you fail to address them? Remember you are trying to identify where you should be focusing your efforts and resources.

Step 6

- For each critical issue highlight the options for managerial action – generate, elaborate and create – don't go for the obvious. This is an important step as frequently people jump for the known rather than challenge existing assumptions about the way things have been done in the past. Think about the consequences of taking various courses of action.
- Consider the mix of HR systems needed to address the issues. Do you need to improve communications, training or pay?
- What are the implications for the business and the personnel function?
- Once you have worked through the process it should then be possible to translate the action plan into broad objectives. These will need to be broken down into the specialist HR Systems areas of:

(1) training
(2) management development
(3) organization development
(4) appraisal

(5) reward
(6) recruitment
(7) manpower planning
(8) communication.

● Develop your action plan around the critical issues. Set targets and dates for the accomplishment of the key objectives.

Step 7

● Implementation and evaluation of the action plans.

The ultimate purpose of developing a human resource strategy is to ensure that the objectives set are mutually supportive so that the reward and payment systems are integrated with training and career development plans. There is very little value or benefit in training people only to then frustrate them through a failure to provide ample career and development opportunities (see Figure 12).

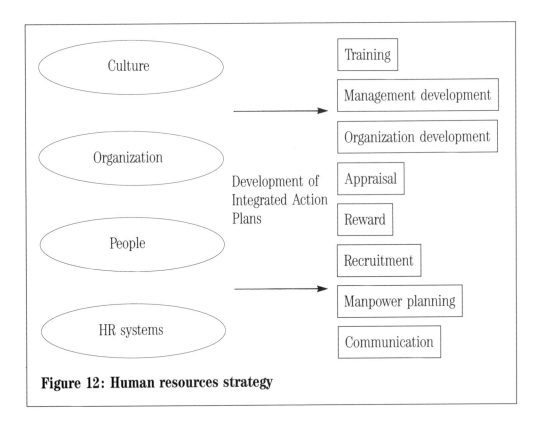

Figure 12: Human resources strategy

8.3 Managing change

The 1990s will require managers to be adept at managing change. Whether it is a change in business direction, major restructuring or a merger or acquisition, managers must manage the change process. Resistance by staff to change is often underestimated and as a result badly handled. Managers are often better trained to deal with the 'what' rather than the 'how' of change. Yet the ability to introduce change with the minimum of resistance is a key managerial skill.

There are five major issues in the management of change:

(1) The difficulty in identifying all the problems likely to arise.
(2) Estimating the amount of time needed to deal with all the difficulties and persuade people to accept the change.
(3) The frequent lack of commitment to the change – the change is desired by 'them' not 'us'.
(4) The impact of new crises which often mean another change in direction.
(5) Time.

1. Why do people resist change?

First of all it should be emphasized that not all changes are resisted. The inclination of staff to oppose change is frequently offset by the possible rewards associated with the change or the prospect of new experiences. Salary increases are generally welcomed but where changes involve interpersonal relationships or the status quo reactions are likely to occur. Indeed where changes are threatened it is frequently the meaning of the change which provokes the resistance. Very often that meaning is distorted by poor communications. Yet the fact that change generates fear is frequently overlooked. Change is always strange and laden with uncertainties even if it is an improvement over the present situation. On a personal level the questions posed are very real.

● Why do we need to change?
● Will I keep my job?
● What will be my new role?
● Will I get a new boss?
● Will they change my department?
● Will they change my title/status?
● What about the future plans for my department?
● Will this damage my career prospects?
● Will I have to move home?
● Can I trust the new management?
● What is in it for me?
● When will the change happen?

During periods of large-scale change such as a company merger or acquisition these types of questions when left unanswered can cause havoc on business performance, as people focus their energies and attention internally rather than on their customers. It also goes unnoticed that these questions are frequently asked by senior managers who themselves are being asked to implement the change. Little wonder that the process of managing change can prove so difficult.

Of course once an organization has started to introduce major change managers must manage further problems which pose even greater pressures on the organization (see Figure 13). The majority of these issues demand considerable planning and even then it is not always possible to convince people of the need for change.

2. The question of corporate culture

In recent years managers have been urged

Figure 13: Managing major change – some common issues

Issues   *Symptoms*

● Role confusion ————————→ 'What am I supposed to be doing.'

'I thought they were responsible for that.'

● Cynicism ————————————→ 'There was nothing wrong with the old way.'

'This is just the flavour of the month.'

● Holding on to the past ————→ 'It was better in the old days.'

● Commitment of senior ———→ 'I'll change when they change.'
management

'I'll believe it when I see it.'

● Skills/knowledge gaps ———→ 'I'm not sure I can do this.'

'I have not been trained to do this.'

● Apprehension ———————→ 'Where am I going to find the time to do this as well.'

● Reversal to the past ————→ 'Oh that – I stopped doing it six weeks ago.'

● Who is responsible for
implementing the changes ——→ 'It's nothing to do with me!'

---

to look at their organization's culture when trying to manage change more effectively. Indeed it is common to hear chief executives talk of the need to change the culture of a business in order to improve performance. Yet despite this level of interest corporate culture still remains, for many managers, undefined.

Perhaps the most useful definition of corporate culture is 'the way we do things around here'. It reflects the management style and atmosphere of an organization. On a more detailed level it is made up of:

(1) *Beliefs and values*:
about the organization and its place in the world, e.g. I believe this organization stands for quality. I think this organization is striving to be the best.

(2) *Norms*:
the behaviour which is generally most acceptable in the organization, e.g. approaches to problem solving, the way meetings are run, use of first names, dress standards, standards of performance required, etc.

(3) *Style*:
the management style and behaviour e.g. open-door, autocratic, paternalistic. The use of rewards and punishment.

Another way of looking at these aspects of culture is to view beliefs and values as existing below the surface of the organization and norms and style as being above the surface. It is obviously difficult to find out what people are thinking about as in the case of their beliefs and values. However, it is relatively easy to identify an organization's management style.

Observing how managers manage and the extent to which standards of performance, quality and customer care are applied tell us much more about the culture of an organization. Consider for example how an organization tackles problems, does it appoint a committee or task an individual with solving the problem? The way meetings are run is also another example of an organization's culture. Some organizations run very open meetings while others have closed and secretive get togethers.

So is culture something that managers should be interested in? The significant point is that *culture can be both an accelerator and a brake on an organization's performance*. To help illustrate this point the model developed by Colin Price at Price Waterhouse is helpful (see Figure 14).

Ultimately any organization is judged by its performance in the market place. In this context perception is the key word. The image of an organization is predominantly shaped by the behaviour of staff. Suppliers, customers, competitors and the media all have a perception of the organization. This perception is developed in many ways. On one level it is the way in which a receptionist answers the telephone or greets visitors. On another it is the manner in which a salesman deals with customers, whether invoices are paid on time or quality goods are delivered on time and to cost. All these interactions with the outside world will help to shape perception.

So perception is shaped by behaviour and that ultimately determines profitability. So what are the ways in which managers try to shape behaviour? Tradi-

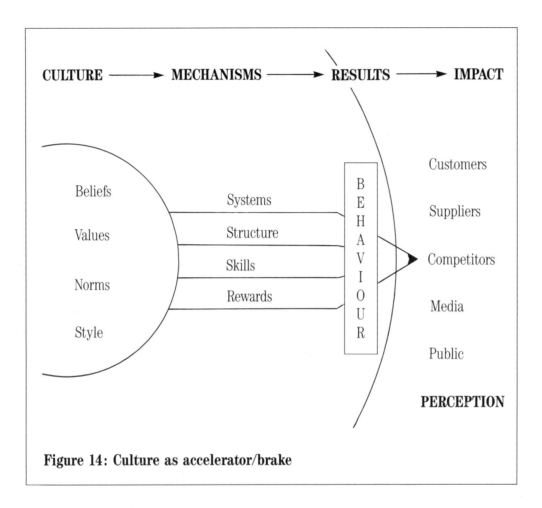

Figure 14: Culture as accelerator/brake

tionally organizations have tried to influence their staff by using a number of levers or mechanisms.

(1) Systems

A change in systems is one of the most favoured aspects of trying to influence people's behaviour. Huge investments in information technology are associated with trying to reduce costs and improve efficiency. It is expected that by providing managers with up-to-date management information they will be able to make faster and more effective business decisions and hence improve business performance and ultimately profitability.

(2) Organization structure

Managers spend a lot of time trying to develop the most appropriate organization structure to manage their business. The arguments over centralization, decentralization, divisionalization and matrix structures are common throughout every organization. Indeed some managers would argue that there have been clear trends as to which structure is in vogue at a particular point in time. Nevertheless, the express intention of changing an organization structure is to effect a change in people's behaviour, either by exerting more control over staff or providing greater autonomy and freedom to managers.

(3) Skills training

A key objective of most skills training is to change behaviour. Customer care, management, inter-personal and technical skills training is aimed at encouraging people to do things differently at the end of the training programme.

(4) Rewards

At the same time changes in pay and reward systems are aimed at redirecting staff behaviour. In the case of production workers it is to improve quality or output. In the sales function changes in commission and incentive schemes are directed at improving sales of a particular product range or to encourage the sale of after sales service contracts or some other new or value added service. The end objective is the same – 'we want you to do something differently'.

The fact is that while these change levers work effectively on many occasions, there are many others where large amounts of money and management time have failed to deliver the required changes in behaviour and subsequent business performance. The reason for these failures can often be attributed to management's failure to pay due attention to the impact of the organization's culture.

Customer care campaigns
– a warning

The 1980s saw enormous interest placed on customer service and care. Inspired by the success of airline organizations such as SAS and British Airways, organizations involved in all sectors from manufacturing through to financial services have endeavoured to emulate their successes. In many instances management have invested heavily only to be disappointed with the results. All too often senior managers frequently failed to recognize the huge amount of management attention and commitment that is required to successfully drive a customer care initiative. Many campaigns became little more than 'smile campaigns' whereby front-line staff were encouraged to smile politely to customers and wear new uniforms. Behind these efforts little work was done to address more fundamental issues relating to the product's quality or internal management systems because there was a failure to understand the need to change the culture of the business.

If we look at the British Airways 'Putting People First' campaign we can understand the depth and complexity of their approach. Integrating actions across the spectrum of the organization's, culture, organization, people and systems were taken. These included:

- a shake out of senior management
- the introduction of performance management structures
- huge investment in training
- wide-ranging customer care initiatives
- large scale re-organization
- the real commitment of senior management.

The last point is perhaps the most important of all. Very little culture change will occur in any organization unless senior management understands the reason for the changes and are committed to it. The fact that Colin Marshall as Chief Executive of British Airways attended the majority of staff seminars on customer care has become part of the British Airways success legend. His actions and highly visible support left the organization in no doubt that the company was serious about the initiative and that a commitment to quality had to become a fundamental belief in the business.

3. How to change your corporate culture

Frequently managers ask if there is a good and bad culture to have. The fact is that there is no right or wrong culture to have. Every organization has a culture whether management thinks consciously about it or not. The real question is whether the culture matches the strategy of your organization.

Ultimately corporate culture must be constantly tuned to the business strategy and environment.

The risks of having a strong culture are:

● *Obsolescence –*
the culture becomes outdated, the market-place moves or a new competitor enters which results in a mismatch between your strategy and culture.

● *Resistance –*
the culture inhibits change; core values and beliefs can be extremely difficult to change.

Clearly therefore changing an organization's culture is not an easy task. While there are many people who put forward 'quick fix' solutions most managers who have been involved in culture change agree that it takes years rather than months to effect a lasting change. Indeed some would argue that it is a continuous

process which managers must never let up on.

The essential prerequisites for successful culture change are:

(1) a clear sense of direction or vision as to what the new organization wants to achieve
(2) the clear commitment and ownership of top management to the change
(3) the ability to manage people's expectation. Not everything changes overnight and managers and staff need to be prepared for set backs
(4) an effective communications programme which emphasizes the role of middle managers and staff in the change process and secures their commitment and ownership to the changes.
(5) the commitment of resources to train staff.

Remember, in the long-term people are more interested in how managements behave rather than what they say. Developing fancy statements relating to an organization's mission or sense of customer care is relatively easy. It is actually delivering the words that is the difficult part of the process. Behaving and managing in a way which is consistent with what is being said can be very painful for some managers!

4. How to manage change

● *Cultivate an appetite for change.* If changes are frequent they will be more acceptable. People will be used to the idea of change if they come to see it as a common aspect of work.

- *Provide trust*. Much depends on the degree of confidence and trust which employees have in management. There is a need to build up trust and strong working relationships over a long period.
- *Watch the timing*. Take time in introducing change, create a favourable atmosphere, give people time to get accustomed to an idea before implementing it. There are few occasions when the quick introduction of change without prior notice will work.
- *Give information*. Keep people informed, give the full reasons for the change. Provide full and accurate information. Highlight the benefits of the change.
- *Do not expect instant conversion*. Gain participation in decision-making. This develops commitment to the decision. Talking at people gives them an awareness, but mutual decision-making results in far more acceptance and ownership.
- *Avoid using too many arguments* – stick to the essentials.
- *Avoid criticism of the past*; concentrate on positive aspects of the change, and a desire to make progress.
- *Ask questions* that will concentrate the discussion on areas of agreement.
- *Aim at an acceptable solution*, not necessarily a 100 per cent conversion.
- *Listen sympathetically* to problems and objections but avoid assumptions that the ojections stated are necessarily the real ones; they may hide objections which the person does not want to admit.
- *Be wary of 'negative suggestions'*, i.e. 'It would be fine if we could do so and

so, but it is not really possible in a firm like ours.'
- *Assume that acceptance has been won* and stress the advantages and benefits while admitting the difficulties. Suggest that the inevitable change are problems can be overcome. Ask for advice on how to overcome the more obvious problems.
- *Emphasize continued support* and help both during and after the change.
- Once agreement seems reasonably certain, *get the plans agreed quickly* including a programme and timetable.
- *Give others a share of the credit* for the change.
- *Provide re-training* where applicable. Try to have a clear-cut policy or procedure.
- Finally *remember that to be logically right can be psychologically wrong*.

5. How to plan the introduction of change

The wheel technique (see figure 15)
(1) identify the *objective* you wish to achieve by introducing the change.
- The more specific the *objective* is the easier it is to define techniques for its achievement.
- An example might be: 'To improve the output of a work group from 70 to 80 per cent of what is theoretically possible.'
- Note that the objective can be an intermediate (but practical) step to a more desirable goal. Thus a safety officer's objective of ensuring that every employee wears a safety helmet might be achieved through a series of more realistic stages, e.g. 'To ensure that

management wears safety helmets.'

(2) Write the *objective* (in an abbreviated form) in the centre of a piece of paper.

(3) Draw out from the centre 'spokes' to form a wheel (there is no limit to the number of 'spokes' to form a wheel).

(4) List individuals or groups into the 'spokes':
- These are people who will be affected by the proposed change (directly or remotely).
- You must also include those people who can influence the change, by their support, their acquiescence, or their opposition.
- There are no special rules about whether a person should be singled out and placed in a 'spoke' on his own, or put in with a group. The key question is whether the individual has power – the power to assist or impede the change.

(5) Look again at your objective.
- Specify in as much detail as possible the situation you would like to exist when your objective is achieved, including a time-scale for accomplishment.
- Is the objective still realistic? If there is some doubt in your mind, can you take action to make the objective more realistic?

(6) Identify the separate responses from each 'spoke'. At this stage the likely response can be indicated in very broad terms: approval, opposition, or indifference.

(7) Look for 'Levers'
- In any 'spoke' there may be one or several people who have some power to influence (positively or negatively) the desired change.
- Such people or 'levers' may perform very ordinary roles in the organization, but are invested with power because of the nature of the desired objective, e.g. a manager who leans heavily on the advice of his personal assistant, or a reprographic operator whose co-operation is essential if documents are to be printed and distributed in time.
- It is worthwhile to contact such people as they can provide feedback about the likely perception of your proposed change by other people.

(8) Select the *priority* 'spokes'. Such 'spokes' may be in a powerful position for influencing other 'spokes', or possibly the strength of their opposition to the change is such that some action needs to be taken.

(9) Consider the inter-relationship of each 'spoke'. It can sometimes reveal new approaches to the problem of implementing change if you look at each 'spoke' in turn as it is influenced by other 'spokes' or influences them.

(10) Analyse the driving and restraining forces in the first *priority* 'spoke'.
- Take a fresh piece of paper and draw a horizontal line across the middle to represent the equilibrium between you and the attitudes within that 'spoke'.
- The driving forces are the arguments and opinions in favour of the change.
- The restraining forces are the arguments and opinions against the change.

- Clearly you are sometimes wrong about both the actual factors that constitute driving forces, as well as the real strength behind each restraining force. Your accuracy depends on trial and error, plus accumulated experience.
- Try to estimate the relative importance of each of the restraining forces by giving each a score between 1 (low) and 10 (high).

(11) Devise an *action plan* to remove or minimize the restraining forces.

- Now you can begin to design a strategy for change that has taken account of all the major people and groups involved, and the type of resistance likely to be encountered.
- Generally, it is preferable to remove (or minimize) the restraining forces that increase the strength of the driving forces. If you simply do the latter, you may achieve your objective, but it will cost you an increased level of resistance and tension for which ultimately you (or somebody else) will pay.
- The process of removing or reducing the restraining forces may take weeks, months or years in the case of major cultural change.
- This is the really difficult part of the process of introducing change. There are no easy ways of overcoming a person's sense of outraged pride, or of helping someone to accept a loss of status or autonomy.

(12) *Caution*

- The 'wheel technique' only represents one person's view of the situation. There is plenty of scope for error: you can never be sure you have correctly identified all the persons or groups with influential views on the proposed change.
- Even if your 'wheel', or your force field diagrams of driving and restraining forces, are accurate when they are drawn, the situation can change.

Force field analysis for a 'priority spoke'

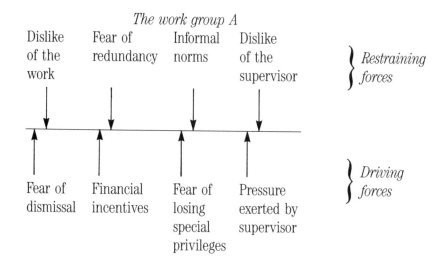

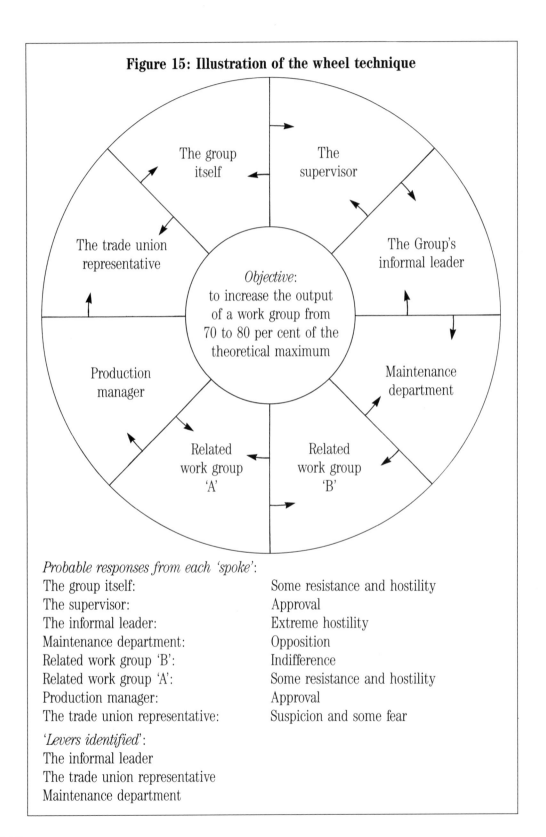

Figure 15: Illustration of the wheel technique

Probable responses from each 'spoke':

The group itself:	Some resistance and hostility
The supervisor:	Approval
The informal leader:	Extreme hostility
Maintenance department:	Opposition
Related work group 'B':	Indifference
Related work group 'A':	Some resistance and hostility
Production manager:	Approval
The trade union representative:	Suspicion and some fear

'Levers identified':
The informal leader
The trade union representative
Maintenance department

The balance of the equilibrium can be changed by

- removing or reducing the *restraining forces*
- increasing (or adding to) the *driving forces*.

Warning

Overall the strategy for increasing (or adding to) the driving forces does tend to succeed because management works very hard, applies pressure, and knocks a few heads together (removing some, if necessary!), but it can also create resisting forces which are costly to organizational efficiency and flexibility in the long run.

- The whole technique concerns itself solely with strategy: it does not deal with face-to-face persuasion or the detailed implementation of change.
- Your portrayal of any given force field may itself omit significant elements, or you may misjudge the strength of any particular factor.

8.4 Communications

An essential element of effective people management is the ability of senior management to communicate effectively with their staff. Companies who communicate with and involve their staff are rewarded with a motivated workforce, greater commitment to the organization and support for management actions.

Some of the strategic factors that are involved in attempts to improve communications include:

- increasing competition and the consequent need to convey business realities
- changes to the culture and structure of the business
- the need for increased staff co-operation, innovation and ideas
- the need for greater flexibility and efficiency.

On a more technical level the aims of communicating within an organization can include to:

- inform
- instruct
- persuade
- negotiate
- advise
- maintain discipline
- challenge
- motivate
- build a team
- involve
- inquire.

People primarily want to know about their organization's plans for the future and how well they are performing in their job. To that extent information that is communicated to staff should be checked against the following needs. Messages should be:

- accurate
- clear
- relevant
- meaningful
- timely

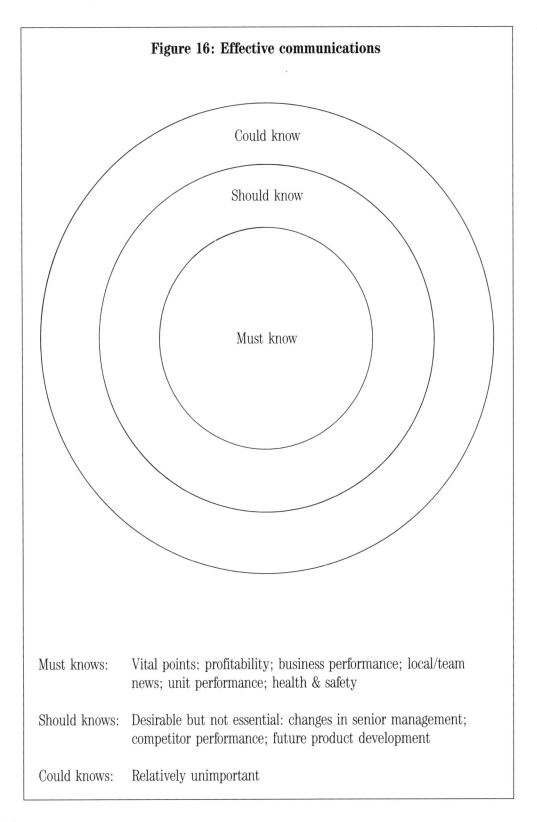

Figure 16: Effective communications

Could know

Should know

Must know

Must knows: Vital points: profitability; business performance; local/team news; unit performance; health & safety

Should knows: Desirable but not essential: changes in senior management; competitor performance; future product development

Could knows: Relatively unimportant

- reliable
- credible.

At the same time senior managers might like to consider the must, should and could knows for staff (see figure 16).

Communications channels

Nowadays many organizations have recognized the need to encourage staff to provide ideas and suggestions for improving business performance. At the same time senior managers are seen to consult people on issues that directly affect them. In terms of the channels used to convey messages the choice has never been greater:

- office notice boards
- weekly bulletin sheets
- staff handbooks
- formal team briefings
- informal discussions
- audio/video cassettes
- memoranda
- staff meetings
- electronic mail
- company journals/newspapers
- trade unions
- media – press and TV
- grapevine

Remember, the *message* is more important than the *medium*. Many expensive corporate videos have failed because the medium appeared more important than the message.

Two-way communication is always preferable to one-way. As a result face-to-face briefings and discussions between managers and staff are the most effective medium of communication. Even so the success of such briefings again relies upon the quality of the information and the message being given.

The speed with which a message is delivered is also an important part of the process. There is little point in communicating something that most people already know about. The grapevine continues to remain an important channel of communication in most organizations. In certain instances it is very difficult to beat the grapevine for speed. However, staff, while acknowledging the role of the grapevine, frequently distrust the accuracy of this medium. In the majority of cases people prefer to get their information direct from management.

In reviewing communications, managers must address the areas identified in figure 17. At the same time any changes in communications must be regularly reviewed. Organizations will have many operational pressures and problems which require special approaches. Shift-working alone can cause considerable problems in trying to get a consistent and speedy message across.

While there has been a large move in organizations towards staff briefings there is practical evidence to suggest that where such schemes are not continually supported by top management they quickly fall into disrepair. While company size and resources inevitably make an impact, management commitment and the provision of appropriate training in communications emerge as the critical success factors.

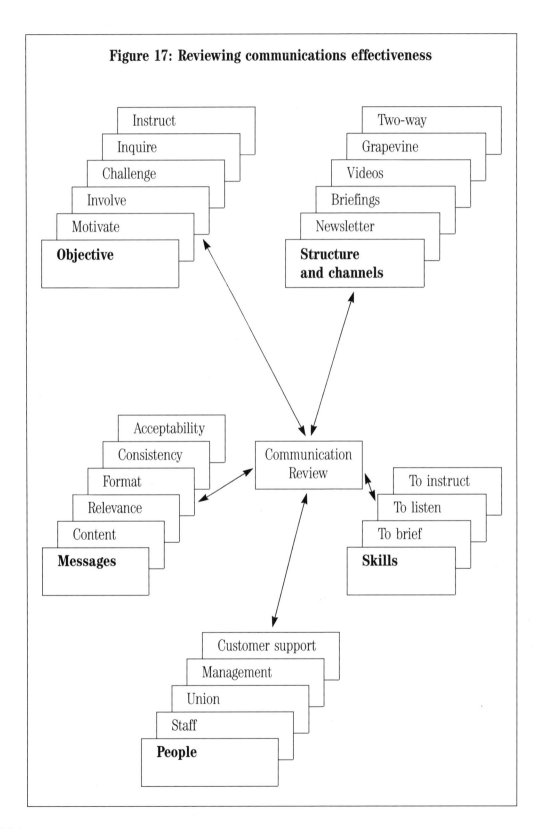

Figure 17: Reviewing communications effectiveness

8.5 Achieving effective people performance — review and appraisal

1. What is it?

Few activities create more emotion, worry and confusion than performance review and appraisal.

This is a pity because in many organizations the performance review and appraisal is a helpful and positive activity which promotes a good working relationship.

What is the difference? It is often the case that in some organizations someone has designed a form or a procedure, issued it and said, 'From the first of next month, there shall be performance reviews'. In the second kind of organization, review and appraisal methods have been developed with the people involved. The worries and fears have been recognized and talked through, and the review methods themselves are reviewed regularly. Above all, everyone involved is aware of the purpose of the activity: to provide an opportunity for the individual and the manager, to access and review how well they are meeting the business needs, now and in the future.

2. Why do it?

The effective performance of people in an organization depends on two processes working in parallel:

● the matching of individuals in terms of skill, knowledge and interest to current and anticipated job demands
● the development of job activities to match the skills and interests of the individuals doing them.

These processes are sometimes in conflict, but a good manager succeeds in balancing any conflicts.

The major part of a manager's job is monitoring, developing and maintaining the balance for the team. Good managers do this as part of their day-to-day management, delegation and supervision.

But an effective employee is not just a 'skill-tap', turned on and off by management. He also checks and develops his own skills and interests against the job demands.

Like all self-regulating, self-controlling systems, both the manager and the employee need clear goals and feedback to be successful. Although they may work together on a continuing basis, it can only help to take 'time-out' from the day-to-day pressures to check on the goals and give each other the feedback and guidance in a sensible relevant way.

The review process should be dealing with questions like:

● 'What am I doing right?'
● 'What am I doing wrong?'
● 'How can I do it better?'
● 'Do I need to change?'
● 'How can you help me?'

The answers need to be based on evidence if they are to be useful and so the focus of the review needs to be job performance and not personal characteristics.

3. Purposes

In more detail, the purposes of review and appraisal can focus on the individual and the organization.

(1) Individual
A wide range of important individual needs are met in the review if the following things happen and the employee is able to continue and comment on them.

- he is made aware of the organization's evaluation of him
- reasons for both success and failure are analysed
- future job plans and programmes are worked out
- career plans and opportunities are discussed
- training and development needs and goals are identified and discussed.

(2) Organization
At the same time, information can be collected which will meet a number of organization needs. These are:

- checking the effectiveness of recruitment and selection procedures
- assessing development programmes
- evaluating previous promotion decisions
- identifying talent
- manpower and succession planning
- development of business plans
- information for salary decisions.

In the long run, a good information system for these activities is in the interests of the organization.

4. How to do it?

Well-designed forms can achieve two main purposes for both the manager and employee:

- giving a basis of comparison between individuals
- focusing attention on relevant points and issues for the interview.

In all cases an interview is essential. It may be tempting to think that a cup of coffee and a 'chat' in the canteen is the best setting for a review. Experience shows, however, that difficult issues are usually avoided in this sort of setting and the conversation can be easily diverted. A relaxed but serious interview is far more useful for both manager and employee. It also underlines the fact that this is 'work' and not a side-issue.

5. Interviews

But interviewing is not easy. It involves verbal and mental skills that need learning and practice. A good performance review needs collaboration and work by both the interviewer and interviewee. The responsibility for a good review not only rests with the interviewer, so guidelines for the manager should be noted by the interviewee as well. A few useful ones are:

- both parties prepare separately by thinking through what has been happening in the job and what you see happening in the future
- think of the review as a joint problem-solving session, not a cross-examination
- prepare a framework or plan of topics

you want to cover
- support your comments with evidence from the job; do not let it become an opinion-trading exercise
- discuss and agree what has happened before moving on to 'good-bad' evaluation
- analyse success as well as failure
- do not make rash promises to avoid discussing a difficult area
- from time to time 'think' yourself into the other person's position, it often helps the problem solving.
- move to agreed plans of action.

Most of the responsibility for moving the interview along rests with the manager and these hints may help.

- state and agree the purpose of the review
- remember the interviewee is 'telling his story' so listen to it
- do not tell him what he *should* be thinking; he is telling you what he *is* thinking
- ask for and listen for his views before expressing your own
- encourage the interviewee to contribute as much as possible to problem solutions and action plans. Remember they are his problems and plans and he may know the job better than you.

6. Seven deadly sins

The form of words and face-to-face skills of doing this demand thought and practice but some common sins and cures are:

'What have you been doing?'
The manager should know.

'I think you're lazy.'
So what? Does it affect the job?

'Of course, you've sprung this on me.'
Prepare thoroughly.

'Those things are good, so we'll leave it. That's terrible, why?'
Analyse success and failure.

'That may be so, but what you don't know is . . .'
Don't trump aces.

'Well, that's it for another year.'
It shouldn't be. Reviews help the day-to-day process, they don't displace it.

'I haven't really the time for this.'
What are you doing if you don't have time to review your employees' work and development? Employees are probably ineffective and managers are not managing.

8.6 Human resources and your organization

The following check-lists present some questions which may prove helpful as you think about your organization.

Since check-lists are not exhaustive, you should treat them as open-ended. Therefore use them to provoke thought and to stimulate discussion rather than as an end in itself. They will help you to identify the critical human resource issues facing your organization.

The aim is to begin to explore how a considered and planned approach to people management can improve business performance.

1. Business strategy and human resource management

'Panic points' check-list

Warning signs of an organization in trouble:

- chronic industrial relations problems
- no means of resolving employee grievances
- increasing/erratic employee turnover
- increasing number of customer complaints
- no pride in the organization
- top team conflicts
- dissatisfaction with pay and conditions
- unclear job roles
- no clear performance measures
- quality is unimportant
- bad product service/delivery records
- poor recruitment standards/practices
- no management development programmes
- no induction training for new employees
- critical skill shortages
- inter-departmental warfare.

2. Culture, organization, people, systems (COPS)

Culture   *Comments*

- Do your staff identify with the organization and 'the success of the organization' as being of direct benefit to themselves?
- Do your staff see themselves as having common interests with their work colleagues and group? Is there a strong team spirit?
- Is work allocated on the basis of individual expertise rather than position in the organization?
- Are your staff encouraged to say what they think about the organization?
- Does your organization encourage innovation and creativity amongst staff?
- Do your staff feel a sense of personal responsibility for their work?
- Is quality emphasized in all aspects of the organization?

Organization

Comments

- Does the structure of your organization encourage effective performance?
- Is the organization structure flexible in the face of changing demands?
- Is the structure too complex? If so in what areas?
- Do your staff have clear roles and responsibilities?
- Does your organization structure tend to push problems up rather than resolve them at the point where they occur?
- Do your procedures and management practices facilitate the accomplishment of tasks?
- Do you constantly seek to challenge your organization structure?

People

- Do your staff have the necessary skills and knowledge to perform their jobs in the most effective manner?
- Do your staff understand their jobs and how they contribute to overall business performance?
- Do your staff have a customer service orientation?
- Are people with potential spotted and developed for the future?
- Are your staff encouraged to perform well through the giving of recognition, feedback, etc?
- Do your people know what their expected performance standards are?

Systems

- Do your organization's systems (e.g. recruitment, promotion, planning, management, information and control) encourage effective performance among your staff?
- Are these systems consistent across the organization?

● Are there clear rewards for effective performance within your work group?

● Does the organization review its systems frequently and ensure they mutually support each other?

Consider

(1) What are the three critical people issues facing your business?

    (a)

    (b)

    (c)

(2) What plans/actions are you taking to address them?

3. Identifying training needs

An employee in your department, division or organization is not doing what they should be doing. So ask yourself some basic questions:

(1) ● Why is the performance unsatisfactory?

    ● What events cause you to say things are not right?

    ● Are you clear what the individual should be doing?

(2) ● Could the job be better carried out in some other way?

    ● Is it possible to change the job?

    ● Would you be allowed to?

    ● What do you have to do to change it?

If a change in performance is necessary consider the following questions. Is the problem

● related to the work being carried out?

● personal to the individual?

First, consider '*related to the work carried out*':

(1) ● Is the work rewarding the achievement of performance?

    ● Does the individual feel that achieving the desired performance is 'too much effort'?

    ● What satisfaction (e.g. perks, prestige, leisure time) does the individual get out of his present performance?

    ● Are you rewarding irrelevant and overlooking critical behaviour?

    ● Can you change the rewards?

(2) ● Would retraining be acceptable and desirable?

    ● Will training adequately meet the development needs?

    ● What training could you recommend be undertaken?

    ● If the individual does not develop, what will happen?

(3) ● What are the obstacles to development?

    ● Does the individual know what is expected in terms of performance and delivery?

    ● Does the individual lack the authority or the time or the resources?

    ● Is there a 'right way of doing it' or a 'way we've always done it' which ought to be changed?

    ● Can you reduce the demands of less

important but more immediate problems?

Now consider what is '*personal to the individual*':

(1) ● Has the individual got the ability?
 ● What are the physical and mental qualities necessary to do the job?
(2) ● Has the individual ever done the job adequately?
 ● Has the job changed?
 ● Has the individual forgotten how to do it?
 ● Is some refresher training called for?
 ● Is feedback provided about how the job should be done?
(3) ● Does the individual have to do this particular job or use this ability often?

● Would more practice help?
(4) ● Is there a positive attitude to getting the job done and to developing?
 ● Has this attitude changed recently?
 ● How much do I know about the needs and personal motivations?

So, what should I do now?

● Are some solutions inappropriate or beyond our resources?
● Which remedy will require the most/least effort?
● Which remedy is most likely to succeed?
● Which are we best equipped to try?
● Is it worth it – what would it 'cost' and what would be the benefits if it proved successful?

Competitive Marketing Strategy

9.1 The purpose of strategy

Successful marketing strategy is at the core of a company's ability not just to market its goods or services but also to develop new products or services successfully and to maintain increased profitability.

To achieve our objectives we need above all to be keenly aware of where we stand in relation to both our customers and our competitors, hence the title of this chapter.

'Strategy' is a concept which is frequently misused. Here are some examples – definitions taken from actual business meetings in which strategy was being discussed – of what it is not.

Strategy is *not*

- a plan to produce 20 per cent growth in earnings per share
- this is a by-product of successful strategy
- a decision to divest underperforming assets or product lines
- this is an action which frees up resources to allow strategy to be pursued in other areas
- acquiring, e.g. XYZ companies in Europe
- acquisitions are actions that should result from strategy and not vice versa.

Acquisitions and divestments do not represent strategy, though they may result from clearly thought-through strategy.

What, then, is strategy? Strategy *is*

- selecting markets and market segments in which to compete
- providing a mix of products and services that customers value
- doing it all better – or for lower cost – than your competitors.

And why is strategy so important? It is the interaction of customer *needs* and competitive *offerings and costs* which determines:

- who makes the sale
- and at what profit.

The essence of strategy is to identify business areas in which we can achieve a competitive edge. Why is concentration on competitive edge so important? It's not just a question of offering a better product or service, or even offering these at a lower cost. We also need to provide this value to our customers at a cost to ourselves which will clearly result in profit. This sounds obvious but is often not focused on clearly enough.

We also need to build a *structural* competitive advantage in order to *maintain* our differential edge. IBM's competitive advantage, for example, is its much-vaunted ability to solve all sorts of computer-related problems. It can do this because it has successfully established the type of technical, service and distribution resources required – i.e. the structure is in place.

In order to identify those areas of growth where we can best build and match our competitive advantage to our customers' needs, we need to:

- think of planning in competitive,

relative terms
- ask ourselves, when looking at market growth, not just *what* has happened but *why?*

Think about a particular product in your own business.

- What has driven its growth?
- What is going to happen next?

Look at the Japanese in the 1960s: they successfully anticipated the need to replace the 1940s built cargo ships still mainly in use by most industrialized nations. They were first to fill this market need, and from that point moved into the still more profitable business of building oil tankers.

Now set out – in order of weighting – your own customers' criteria for buying your product or service, e.g.

- availability
- reliability
- price
- service

- technical details
- spares price
- identity.

You can then draw various conclusions. For example, recent research into the purchase criteria employed in the control and instrumentation industry showed that:

- technical back-up was seen as very important for large projects, but not at all for small projects
- price was important for wholesalers of small projects but much less so for small projects end-users
- delivery speed was crucial for users of small projects and almost immaterial for large projects.

Remember when conducting research:

(1) be sure that your sample is a good cross-section
(2) structure your questions properly to ensure you find out what your customers really think.

9.2 Market segments: from sharks to piranhas

Sometimes differing demands will emerge within the same market, i.e. the market has split into more than one, it has segmented. If you have a cluster of people with a significantly different set of demands, that is a segment.

How can we supply our product/service better than our competitors, and at a lower cost, for differing sets of needs and requirements? The answer is to establish a niche marketing strategy. Build your competitive advantage in a specific segment, in other words become a piranha, not a shark.

There are a myriad customer needs. Creating fresh segments (finding particular groups, particular needs) can be a test of your own creativity.

Go back to your own customers' *key purchasing criteria*. Now break down your market into two segments and work out how the criteria will vary in each.

For example, a manufacturer of outside camera mounting equipment segments his market into professional and amateur:

Rating	*Professional*
1	Weight
2	Technical performance
4	Availability
3	Quality/ Reliability
5	Price

Rating	*Amateur*
4	Weight
5	Technical performance
2	Availability
3	Quality/ Reliability
1	Price

If he gets weight and technical performance right, he will clearly win in the professional market, but not of course in the amateur market, where price and availability are the key factors.

Another way of looking at the competition is to list weighted key purchase criteria (which you will have established through your research) and then allocate points between yourself and your competitor.

Here is another example: the house-building industry :

Weighted criteria	Us	Them
4 Technical specification	9	8
2 Delivery/programme	9	8
3 Technical service	8	9
1 Price	7	8
5 Quality assurance	10	6

What is happening here? The competition is winning market share through scoring higher on the key criterion of price.

The first rule of strategy is 'Know your adversary'. It is not enough to know what our customers want and which aspects of our product or service they value most highly. We also need to know all about our competition. If we know:

(1) what our customers want
(2) what our competitors are offering

we will then know

(3) which competitor/product is growing/ declining.

Any two of three will give us the other piece of information.

It is always important to compare competitor ratings for key purchase criteria to obtain a clear picture of

● competitors' marketing strategy
● their chances of growing or declining in the market

You should measure your competitor's response/performance in relation to various key purchase criteria, e.g. delivery, service, price, quality, technical support, credit, spares availability, and so on.

In comparing competitor ratings, your analysis might for example reveal the following:

- *Competitor A* goes for a 'pile 'em high, sell 'em cheap' policy. Availability is not all that good, but quality is reasonable. Survives on price advantage alone.
- *Competitor B* takes the 'Marks and Spencer' approach and scores consistently well, especially on quality. By no means the cheapest, but doesn't have to be, because of sound reputation.
- *Competitor C* goes for top quality in terms of service and technical support, and easily beats the rest of the field. Clear competitive edge in these two key areas.
- *Competitor D* could well be in trouble. (Sell the shares if you're still holding them!) Trying to do everything but hasn't scored significantly on anything.

What do you do if price is a major criterion and you are being beaten?

- examine your costs and pricing structure
- if you cannot reduce costs – or do not choose to – look at where you can add value.

This is a situation where you may well have to test your creativity in finding a new segment where price is not the key factor. But note that, clearly, it may not be possible to attack a new segment without putting fresh strain on existing resources, e.g. technical, production, promotion or distribution. In which case, think again.

The first thing to do is to decide how you wish to segment the market in question and which criteria to use. You can construct a very simple set of criteria, or a more complex set of variables,

depending on the situation.

Typical criteria would be as follows:

- demographic
  - age
  - sex
  - occupation
  - income
  - education
  - socio/economic group (A, B, C1, C2, etc.)
- customer behaviour
  - usage (non-user, light/heavy user)
  - benefits sought (economy, status)
  - marketing factor sensitivity (quality, price, service etc.)
- geographic
  - region
  - density (urban, rural)
- behavioural
  - political (radical, conservative, liberal)
  - social (assertive, non-assertive)
  - ambition (ambitious striver, low-achiever)
  - autonomy (dependent, independent).

The variables above are only examples of the many criteria you can use. They may or may not be important, but the exercise of thinking through which variables matter is in itself of great value. It can also be creative, in establishing a potential new market segment.

- It is up to you which criteria you select; these will vary depending on the product/markets.
- There may be little or no segmentation under certain main headings (e.g. geographic) and a great deal of seg-

mentation within others (e.g. benefits sought).

- Be consistent in your research, i.e. the questions you ask.
- Always ensure you take a representative sample.
- Re-check your assumptions through further research, e.g. via your sales force.

9.3 Costs and market share

1. The experience curve

A great deal has been written in the last two decades about business strategy in a competitive marketing context. Theories of market share and new product development have been invented and refined. In essence, the classic theory is:

- market share relative to the competition helps to create scale – this is known as the 'experience curve'
- the 'experience curve' reduces costs
- market share is therefore the key to increased profits.

Put another way, costs are a function of accumulated volume; high market share

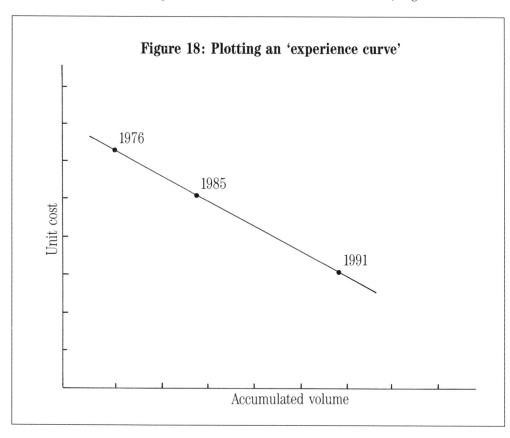

Figure 18: Plotting an 'experience curve'

can yield low costs and high profits; and products should be managed differently, as a function of their relative market share and market growth, to achieve high product/market shares relative to competition (see Figure 18).

Remember when dealing with market share:

(1) It is important to be very clear about which market or markets you are talking about.

(2) The key words are 'relative to the competition', i.e. your volume, your costs and your pricing are a function of the *realizable* market in relation to your competition.

2. The product portfolio

The theory goes on to say that products should be managed differently – especially

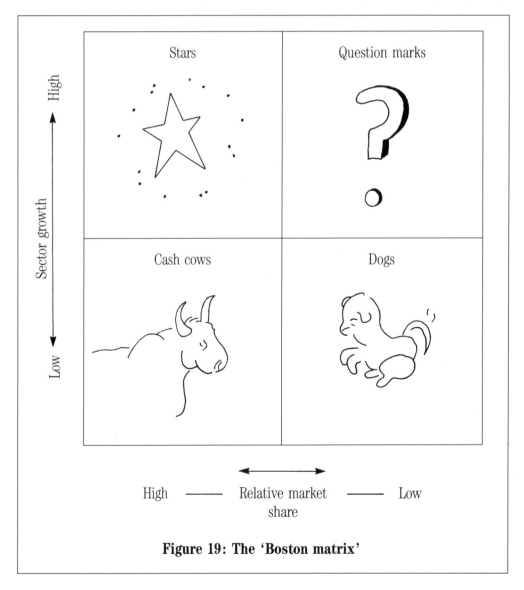

Figure 19: The 'Boston matrix'

from an investment point of view – depending on where they stand in relation to:

- relative market share
- market growth.

Out of this theory emerged the now famous 'Boston matrix' (see figure 19) which graphically demonstrates the relative position of a group of products within a company. It introduced a menagerie of terms: stars, cash cows, dogs and question marks.

- *Stars*: High relative market share, in a growing market: likely to need further investment.
- *Cash cows*: Dominant market position in a declining or static market: needs careful maintenance.
- *Dogs*: Little or no sector growth, and no real market share: disinvest.
- *Question marks*: Low market share in an expanding market creates the problem child. Re-think.

The matrix is divided simply into four; you can, if you wish, sub-divide it by breaking down each side into, say, ten units. This will give you a more refined view, e.g. one of your stars might be nearer the centre in terms of both sector growth and relative market share – the investment decision then is not so simple. Generally, though, this is a simple and effective matrix to clarify initial thinking on product portfolios.

- Do not over-invest in your stars. Put in whatever is necessary to sustain growth.

- Do not over-work your cash cows until they wither – for example by starving them of promotional support.
- Problems thrown up by dogs and question marks – and even cash cows for that matter – might well be solved by further thought on fresh market segmentation strategies.

3. The product life cycle

The product life cycle (see Figure 20) forms a key part of traditional business strategy. Quite simply, it traces the volume and rate of growth of a product over *time*.

It is clearly important in linking *growth* in market share to specific periods of *time*.

Watch out for the period required for *replacement* product demand to come through. It tends to take time, e.g. PCs or electric typewriters.

So beware of market saturation, be concerned about replacement as well as market penetration. Remember the electric slicing knife: how many people use one now?

Look not just for growth and market share, but *sustainable market share*. The 'experience curve' shows that as a company gains experience in manufacturing a product, costs go down. It's all to do with *scale*.

The Honda company experience and the development of the Japanese steel industry are an interesting case in point:

- Japanese steel pours into the west in the 1950s
- result: steel prices in the west go up, in the east they go down
- product development goes from construction to ships to cars

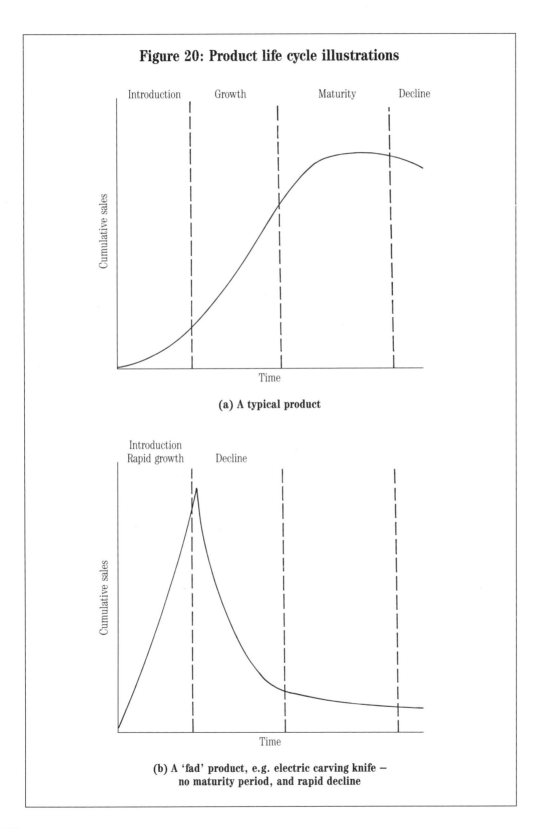

Figure 20: Product life cycle illustrations

(a) A typical product

(b) A 'fad' product, e.g. electric carving knife —
no maturity period, and rapid decline

● further product development via motor-cycles and cars to pumps, out-board motors and lawn-mowers.

9.4 Revenues and costs: the activity-based approach

Our overall objective is always to *maximize the difference between revenues and expenses*. But we can go further in trying to establish the link between products, market share, costs and profits.

Previous thinking has been very *product-based*. We need to switch our attention to *activity*. Why?

● The product-based approach looks at different products in relation to their sales revenue and the market position which the firm enjoys.
● An activity-based approach looks at the activities involved within the firm, e.g.:
  – technology/design
  – production/components
  – sales force
  – promotion expenditure
  – service/technological back-up.
● There is an assumption sometimes that there is a separate 'experience curve' for each product in a company. This is invariably wrong: most companies are more complex than this, with products that are *not* independent in terms of activity or economics.

It is important to show how the different *activities* in the business match with the firm's product lines. How do we achieve cost advantage by activity? We need to understand:

● the dual perspective of our firm, i.e.
  – the marketing position we enjoy in the product/market segment we are in
  – what is going on inside the firm
● where we are spending the money generated by the firm's activities
● whether the revenues we are creating will exceed those costs
● what is the growth-rate of the activity in the work-place.

Remember:

● There is no such thing as a market-place where costs don't matter.
● You're trying all the time to match your cost advantage with what one or more market segments require.
● It is important to maintain a clear picture of your costs compared to those of your competitors in relation to:
  – materials
  – labour
  – sales and marketing
  – distribution.
● A new area of business development may sound like a great marketing idea, but it may demand a significant change in activity levels. Is it, then, still such a brilliant idea?
● Don't try to get hold of competitors' accounts – you won't learn anything.

● Do ask yourself:
  – what are *my* costs?
  – how do my competitors' costs differ in terms of
    (a) how they produce?
    (b) what they produce?

NB: *What* = design, specification (size, complexity, quality). *How* = input costs, scale, efficiency, technology, location, tax/subsidies, distribution costs.

Establish a basis for analysing activity sharing within the firm. For example, look separately at your marketing and distribution activity:

(1) Can the products share management and support personnel, as well as the same sales force?
(2) Can sales, advertising and promotion activity be directed at the same markets (and market segments), as well as through the same distribution channels?
(3) Do a similar analysis of your distribution and service activities.

Again, in terms of production and plant and process engineering, do the products share common components, suppliers, production facilities, personnel?

You should also draw up a comparison of activity structures between competing firms. Think about competitor cost comparison and work out who has built a significant cost advantage.

A typical cost comparison would compare:

● labour
● materials
● management overheads
● other fixed overheads
● transport
● R&D
● sales and admin

and then

● your margin (revealing your cost advantage and/or price premium)

Remember that you do not have a good plan until you can say 'Here is my cost advantage in providing this value to my market.'

Now write down four or more main activities involved in your business. Then do the same for your main competitor. Estimate where you hold cost advantage, and where you don't.

9.5 Strategy formulation, planning and implementation

Deciding on a good strategy is not the result of a sudden flash of inspiration – it's a *process*. You need:

● data
● analysis
● ideas.

Break your data down into:

● market (size/growth, distribution structure, trends, trade)

- competitor (share/scale, growth, product/service offering, activities/ integration, stated or apparent strategy)
- customer (who are they, what makes them buy, what trends are evident?)

You can find your data through a variety of sources:

- *internal*, e.g. what you know about customer needs, costs, etc.
- *indirect external sources*, e.g. government statistics, industry reports, etc.
- direct external sources, e.g. customer and competitor interviews.

Remember:

- It's better to be approximately right than precisely wrong.
- Don't get analysis paralysis!
- Don't let the numbers take over.

Analysis in strategy formulation should concentrate on:

- what is happening
  - segments and competitors
- why it is happening
  - product/service mix
- what it means for the bottom line
  - value added activities
  - what drives the costs
- the alternatives
  - risk/return.

For ideas on strategy formulation, remember that:

- Good ideas are rarely limited to one person. Go wide. Involve as many people as possible.
- The Japanese tend to discuss strategy in large groups (contrary to practice in the UK). Their strategy formulation is frequently highly successful. Strategy emerges slowly, ideas filter back (often after the meeting) and the firm gains the advantage of spreading its net wide.
- People enjoy talking about their ideas: listen carefully to what your organization, the market place and other external sources are telling you.
- Encourage people to think through and express their own ideas.
- Act: don't lose the momentum.

For the process of strategy formulation:

- *Don't* try to get there in one go; a single meeting is rarely enough.
- *Do* go back, as fresh options emerge, to test your assumptions and re-work the data and analysis before finalizing your strategy.
- *Don't* succumb to the 'short-cut disease'.

Finally, these are the key points to remember for successful strategy implementation:

(1) Be systematic, be patient and be thorough.
(2) Note that strategy formulation is closely connected to strategy implementation.
(3) Ensure that everybody understands what is involved; once the strategy is agreed you can then move rapidly to put it into action.
(4) make sure your operating plans link properly to your strategic plans, e.g. it's no good stating that 'We're going to

be the sector's lowest-cost producer' while budgeting for high labour costs.

(5) Beware of factors which can get in the way of implementation:
- company culture
- perceptions
- habits
- beliefs
- morale
- expectations
- attitudes.

(6) Draw up a schedule of key tasks necessary for implementing your strategy, clarify responsibilities and set time limits.

(7) Monitor progress.

There is nothing academic about the strategy formulation process: it must never be simply an intellectual exercise. Strategy is a coherent action plan.

Good strategy feeds through to the bottom line.

Part 3
Business
Development

Strategy and Business Development

This chapter first of all considers the best ways of developing an effective business strategy and, secondly, looks at the most crucial strategy-in-action area of how to approach the turn-around of a loss-making business.

10.1 A practical approach to development strategy

It is generally accepted that a sound business strategy requires a disciplined approach to build a creative yet commercially realistic plan for development. To do this requires identifying both the *economic* and *service mission*.

Under *economic mission*, the financial issues to be addressed are:

- the funding of the assets that will be required
- the likely profit and cash profile of the business
- the level of financial return that will result.

Under *service mission*, the issues to be addressed are:

- the nature of the product/service and the customer profile (followed through by how to reach the market successfully);
- the way in which the product/service will be provided (followed through by how to operate the business successfully).

The putting together of a *business plan* goes hand-in-hand with, or follows on from, the work carried out in formulating a sound business development strategy. (Business plans are covered in Chapter 11, which should be treated as being complementary to this one.)

Now attention will be focused on the practical ways of developing a business strategy.

1. Essential ingredients

The essential ingredients of strategic management are to:

- plan to spend time on it
- take stock of your
  - market-place
  - business
- adopt a quantum leap approach
- assess strategic options
- demolish obstacles to success.

A business which practises strategic management has:

- a one-page vision statement
- financial performance goals
- defined business development projects
- set strategic milestones for budget year
- created an effective organizational structure
- used strategic management workshops.

2. Developing a strategy

The main elements to be addressed are:

- Assess opportunities to
  - obtain market leadership
  - increase market share
  - create niche markets
  - withdraw from unprofitable situations.
- Assess trends and likely developments from
  - economic climate (effects on customers, currencies, etc.)

- technology advances (e.g. effect on distributors)
- political changes (policies and legislation)
- consumerism (e.g. greening of products)
- social change (e.g. population 'greying').

● Choose attractive market segments and countries for:
  - ease of entry
  - good distribution channels.

● Monitor competitors continuously for:
  - products and services (e.g. perform-ance, design, service, innovation and pricing)
  - name awareness.

● Examine any existing business and your or its strengths and weaknesses in these areas:
  - cost and role of head office
  - marketing and public relations
  - selling
  - customer service
  - design
  - distribution
  - research and innovation
  - production
  - asset management
  - cost reduction
  - financial performance (profits and cash).

● Setting financial performance goals
  - listed companies (earnings per share growth and gearing level)
  - subsidiaries and private companies (return on assets, level of profits, cash generation and return on new investment)
  - consider different rates of return on new investment.

Important ingredients for effective business development include:

● a vision statement
● a quantum-leap approach
● taking stock of the business and its markets
● identifying and evaluating the strategic options available
● organization structure
● business-development projects, with milestones of achievement set
● the use of strategic workshops.

Each of these will now be described.

2. Vision statement

Some managers may be familiar with the term 'mission statement'. A vision state-ment is somewhat different: it should describe the particular company in, say, five years' time. In industries with long lead times, however, such as telecommuni-cations and oil exploration, a longer time-scale will be necessary. The essence is that the time-scale chosen should be long enough to achieve major change.

A vision could be compared to a dream, describing the future success of the com-pany, but with the belief and commitment of the executive team to make it into a reality. The vision should harness and focus the energies of people towards the chosen goals, and set priorities where appropriate.

A vision statement is markedly different from a business plan, which is necessarily detailed and supported by financial schedules. A vision statement should be brief (ideally on one side of an A4 sheet). Senior executives should remind themselves of the goals by referring to it regularly, in contrast to many business plans which may be quickly filed and forgotten about.

A statement should include and set out concisely:

- the *market segments and countries*
  - to achieve, maintain or enhance market leadership in
  - to continue investing in without achieving market leadership
  - to enter, by organic growth or acquisition as appropriate
  - to cut back, rationalize or exit from.
- the *commercial rationale of the company*
  - to describe how the company will be seen by customers and prospective customers as attractively and distinctively different from competitors, for example:
    - (a) all products in our supermarkets will be own-label brand; providing a comparable quality and specification with the leading branded product at a lower price, or better quality at the same price, or wherever possible an innovative product not available elsewhere and priced competitively
    - (b) each do-it-yourself superstore will contain a garden centre, offer a home-delivery service, and provide adequate technical advice for customers upon request.
- *essential policies and qualitative goals* which will be pursued, for example:
  - head office will act as investment banker, be as small as possible, and each subsidiary will be an autonomous business
  - sufficient investment will be made in information technology, or robotics, etc. to provide a competitive advantage in the market-place compared with competitors.
  - wherever possible, each member of staff will be rewarded by an incentive scheme based upon personal achievement.
- *broad financial-performance goals*, for example:
  - a minimum or average percentage increase in earnings per share each year
  - the proportion of total profits to be achieved from a certain market within the next five years
  - the percentage return to be achieved on total operating assets within five years.
- *future ownership* (this is particularly relevant for private companies and professional partnerships), for example:
  - a stock-market listing will be obtained within the next three years
  - a merger with another partnership will be pursued to ensure that adequate technical support is affordable.

(These examples are from actual vision statements. This does not necessarily suggest that these examples are appropriate for other companies to adopt.)

Copies of the vision statement in a business should be restricted to directors, partners and senior executives because it is highly confidential. None the less, the relevant parts of the vision can be communicated orally to management and staff as part of briefing meetings. A vision statement is helpful in recruiting the most talented executives and technical specialists. While it is not appropriate to provide a copy of the vision statement at the selection stage, reference to the vision will demonstrate that the company is committed to success.

4. Quantum leap approach

Belief in and commitment to the achievement of the vision are much more important for success than sophisticated corporate planning techniques. Aspiration and attitude are all important.

In contrast, some managers simply plan to achieve mediocrity, and then do not manage to achieve even this. This is because they have planned for only a modest improvement in results, when this amounts to nothing more than continued mediocrity.

The best managers are committed to achieving a quantum leap in results as a vital part of the vision. A quantum leap is a dramatic improvement, without any significant increase in the commercial risks to be undertaken. Quantum leaps are not achieved in a week or a month, and probably not even in a year. Initiatives can be made during this week, this month and this year, however, which will result in a quantum leap being achieved within the medium term.

The ability to achieve a quantum leap is limited only by the imagination. The results achieved are more likely to fall short of the ambition, rather than exceed it. Imagination alone is not enough.

To achieve quantum leap requires:

- *belief* – that it can and will be achieved
- *commitment* – to make the effort needed to make it happen
- *persistence* – to overcome setbacks and obstacles which will be encountered
- *enthusiasm* – to help motivate people.

The motto might be 'think big and make it happen!' The growth and success of companies such as Hanson Trust, WPP, Nissan, MacDonalds and The Body Shop did not happen by accident. The first step for a small business to become a national or worldwide market leader is for the chief executive to have the vision, belief and total commitment to make it happen.

5. Taking stock

This means taking stock of present performance, comparing it with leading competitors where appropriate, and the market opportunities available. Objective measurement is needed, a comfortable view of performance seen through rose-tinted spectacles is inappropriate.

Facets of performance and market opportunities which should be assessed include:

- actual and forecast percentage market shares
- percentage share of each distribution channel within a market
- attractive opportunities in different market segments and countries
- benefits and performance of each product or service group
- niche market opportunities which exist or could be created, e.g. weekend hotel breaks to cater for special-interest groups such as those interested in

gourmet food, wine tasting, antique collecting, bridge, clay-pigeon shooting, etc.

- gaps in the range of products or services offered
- overall percentage return on operating assets
- pricing and discount structures
- identification of major non-customers, especially in markets where there is a concentration of major customers such as supermarket groups and do-it-yourself superstore chains
- speed of delivery and the provision of after-sales service
- level of warranty claims or complaints, and the speed of handling them
- value of business lost by an inability to supply quickly enough
- opportunities to subcontract services more cost effectively than providing them in-house, such as vehicle-fleet management, staff catering, pension administration, cleaning, physical distribution, specialist tax advice, etc.
- level of research and development expenditure, and the results achieved
- staff retention levels.

The aim of this assessment should be to identify:

- opportunities available within the existing business which should be capitalized upon
- attractive niche markets which can be created out of the existing business
- different market segments and countries which should be entered
- the opportunity or need for selective price changes
- the need to set and to achieve improved

standards of performance and to reduce costs.

6. Strategic options

A quantum leap in achievement requires that the strategic options are identified and evaluated. Furrow management, which is merely pursuing minor variations of the same theme, is the enemy of the quantum leap.

Strategic options need to be identified and evaluated for the overall business and within each major department of the business. For example, strategic options at the corporate level of a listed company may include:

- acquiring a larger company overseas to achieve a significant local market share quickly
- obtaining a stock-market listing in one or more overseas countries in which the company has a substantial business
- obtaining a separate stock-market flotation for a major subsidiary, and retaining an equity stake, which would command a higher price-earnings ratio than the group as a whole
- transferring the freehold properties into a separate company and obtaining a stock-market listing for it
- joining with an overseas competitor to make a bid for a major group, in the face of an unwelcome and hostile bid from a corporate raider.

Strategic options which should be evaluated to improve the marketing efforts of a professional partnership may include:

- recruiting a marketing director from

outside the profession

- producing a corporate brochure for the first time
- appointing a public relations consultancy to obtain press and magazine coverage
- presenting seminars to an invited audience of clients and prospective clients on subjects of topical interest that could create business opportunities
- inviting selected clients and prospective clients to lunch to discuss a subject related in some way to the services provided
- encouraging staff to write technical articles for publication in relevant magazines
- experimenting with arts or sports sponsorship on a selective basis
- establishing personal contact with firms in different professions who are in a position to introduce business.

These examples are not recommendations for general use. The intention is to illustrate the range of strategic options which can be identified and evaluated in most business situations. Furrow management must be firmly rejected, and can be easily done by throwing away a self-imposed mental jacket.

7. Organization structure

The organization structure of a business is important for future success. The effect of organization structure is rarely neutral. It is likely either to help the achievement of the vision, or to hamper progress and to encourage internal politics.

A problem is that organizational changes become necessary or desirable from time to time. So several piecemeal changes may be made to the structure over a period of time. As a result, the organization structure should be reviewed comprehensively about every three years.

There is no such thing as an ideal organization structure, not even within a particular industry. The organization structure needs to be designed to help the achievement of the vision and to reflect the strategic options to be pursued.

Important features to be incorporated in an effective organization structure include:

- the role and added value of the head office clearly defined; and the smallest number of people employed to achieve these
- individual businesses created to serve particular market segments, rather than based upon separate product or service groups which may result in several subsidiaries serving, and even competing for, the same customer
- each business responsible for profit, with control of marketing and selling
- personal accountability for achieving measurable results throughout the business.

When the organization structure has been redesigned to achieve the vision and strategic options selected, the strengths and weaknesses of key individuals should be taken into account. Some changes may be needed to capitalize on the strengths of certain people and to compensate for their weaknesses. The aim must be to produce an organization structure that meets the business need and makes the best use of people. Occasionally, however, it may be necessary to recruit someone externally to fill a newly created key appointment rather than compromise by relying upon candidates from within.

People talk about the loneliness of the chief executive of any business. A real example of this is the creation of a new organization structure. Involving members of the executive team to design a new structure may cause problems arising from self-interest.

Organization change often means that some people will gain in seniority and importance, while others will lose. If the chief executive of a business wants to involve other people, the choice should probably be restricted to the chairman, the group chief executive where appropriate, the personnel director, non-executive directors or outside consultants to guard against vested interests and resistance to change.

8. Business-development projects

Revolution is a dangerous recipe for corporate success. In many businesses, with the severity of competition increasing faster than customer demand, evolution is likely to be equally dangerous. What is more, evolution alone is likely to be totally inadequate to achieve a quantum leap.

A proven way to drive a business forward is to create and vigorously pursue a handful of business-development projects. Each project should be the specific accountability of a member of the board or executive committee. Tangible milestones of achievement should be set to ensure adequate progress within the next 12

months. The capital expenditure, working capital and operating costs connected with each project should be included in the approved annual budget, to ensure that adequate resources will be made available.

The business-development projects should not be restricted to research and development. They should focus on whatever achievement is vital to the achievement of the vision and a quantum leap. Projects could be concerned with any aspect of the business.

For example:

● entry into an overseas market by the appointment of distributors
● a company-wide attack on quality, because sustained and critical comment in the press has seriously affected sales
● the acquisition of a silicon-chip manufacturing company to eliminate the reliance on outside suppliers for circuits which are an essential feature of products made by the company.

Some business-development projects will be long term. They may address opportunities which rely upon future developments in advanced technologies such as artificial intelligence, biotechnology and space-satellite broadcasting. None the less, milestones of progress need to be set and achieved within the next 12 months to ensure that the requisite urgency is maintained. In a business achieving only mediocre results, however, the business-development projects are likely to focus more upon short-term improvement.

9. Strategic workshops

Clearly, the structured approach to business development that has been described requires the commitment and involvement of every member of the board or executive committee. Strategic workshops are a powerful means to achieve this.

A strategic workshop should involve the board or executive committee of the business. The aim is to address those issues which are vital to future success.

These could include the creation of a vision for success; setting the size of the quantum leap to be achieved; taking stock of the business and market opportunities, evaluating strategic options and creating business-development projects.

Strategic workshops should be held away from company offices, to avoid distraction by day-to-day matters. A country-house hotel is a suitable venue. Preferably, the participants will meet for dinner the evening before the workshop commences in earnest. This provides an opportunity for the chief executive to set the scene and ensures that a prompt start will be made in the morning. Two working days is probably the amount of time required to address the agenda of vital issues for success.

Features which help to achieve a productive strategic workshop include:

● an agenda restricted to issues of strategic importance; lesser matters must be ruthlessly excluded
● pre-circulated and concise 'position papers' to provide the background to each item on the agenda
● skilled chairmanship to ensure that people say what they believe, while avoiding excessive personal criticism
● a summary of agreement reached, decisions made and further action

committed, circulated promptly after the workshop.

Strategic workshops:

● create belief and commitment to the achievement of the vision, with a clear sense of collective accountability
● improve teamwork and motivation
● are an effective management-development method to help functional directors and executives to develop a broader outlook on the overall needs of the business.

It is important that the first strategic workshop held in a business is productive, because otherwise people are likely to be less enthusiastic on the next occasion.

Strategic workshops are deceptively complex, and previous experience is valuable. Consequently, some companies have used outside advice on the first occasion to ensure success. A typical role of an outside advisor would be to:

● interview each participant to identify the crucial issues for success that should be part of the agenda
● agree the agenda with the chief executive
● advise upon the format and content of the position papers
● participate during the workshop to ensure that the issues are addressed rigorously, and that positive decisions are taken and further action agreed.

Many large companies use strategic workshops in each separate subsidiary, as well as holding them at group level. Some companies go further, and use strategic workshops within major functions of subsidiary companies selectively. Strategic workshops have been widely used in professional partnerships, restricting attendance either to the management committee of the whole business or the relevant partners in a particular country or regional office.

10.2 Turn-round of a loss-making business

This is a testing ground for strategic thinkers where it is obviously essential to succeed in the short term as well as the long term. It emphasizes that it is no good concentrating on long-term strategy at the expense of very real short-term strategic urgency.

An important way to achieve growth in profits is to turn round loss-making businesses. A surprising number of large companies have one or more subsidiaries making losses at any time. The number of private companies which fail is further ample proof of loss-making businesses. One response is a desire to sell the loss-making business, which is really an attempt to walk away from a situation which is both a problem and an opportunity. Even if a buyer is found, the purchase price is likely to be lower than net asset value. If a loss-making business is sold to the existing management interesting questions are raised. What will they do different from before? Why was this not done at the direction of the group previously? The opportunity is to turn the business into profit before considering selling it, because even if a sale makes sense, it will be easier to achieve and a much higher price should be obtained.

1. Initial action

It must be realized that the turn-round of a loss-making business is unlikely to happen unless a new chief executive is appointed. Yet some groups tolerate losses from the same subsidiary for years before appointing a new chief executive to turn round the business. This is nothing less than costly procrastination. Strategic plans which are really a recipe for 'more of the same', without proposing drastic action, should be rejected. Equally, financial analysis alone will not produce the necessary results.

Almost certainly, the essential first step is to appoint a new chief executive with the authority to take the action needed to turn losses into acceptable profits as quickly as possible.

If there is an immediate cash-flow crisis threatening the survival of the business, then tackling this must be the main priority. Specific action which may be needed as a matter of urgency includes:

- meeting the bank and secured creditors to avoid receivership
- negotiating delayed payment of outstanding major trade creditors wherever possible, while reassuring people that effective corrective action is being taken quickly
- concentrating efforts on the collection of outstanding customer debts
- adopting a selective policy for paying

creditors at least some of the money owed to them, to ensure continuity of essential supplies and services, and to avoid damaging legal action wherever possible.

Then there is a strong case for the newly appointed chief executive to make his or her presence felt. The seriousness of the situation should be brought home by a variety of measures such as:

● terminating the employment of all temporary staff until further notice
 – if this could damage the business, someone is likely to scream loudly enough
● requiring personal approval of all overseas travel
 – the purpose of the visit must justify the expense involved and wherever appropriate the proposed visit schedule should be reviewed before approval is given
● suspending non-essential expense until further notice
 – for example, the employment of contractors to redecorate offices, the replacement of company cars, etc.
● delaying all non-essential capital expenditure for a period
● making all recruitment, including the replacing of existing staff, subject to chief executive approval
● eliminating any lavish entertainment or visible extravagance.

The impact of these measures may be modest in relation to the seriousness of the problems which exist. None the less, they serve to make the point that the decks are being cleared in readiness for tough action to be taken where appropriate.

2. Identifying the causes of losses

The next step is to find out the main causes of the loss. The chief executive needs to talk with each member of the board and other members of the management team. Surprisingly often, the main causes quickly become apparent to someone newly appointed to the company. Possible causes may be:

● overhead costs are excessive in relation to sales volume
● the production cost of the service or product is too high compared with the market price
● there is over-capacity in the industry sector
● the marketing and selling efforts are ineffective and too costly
● product performance and customer benefits are no longer competitive
● poor product quality and reliability have undermined sales
● the need for expensive subcontract work to compensate for internal shortcomings.

Urgent financial analysis should be carried out to confirm some of the main causes of the losses. Aspects which need to be assessed include:

● the marginal profit percentage produced by each product or service group
● major customer profitability
● the break-even point of the business based upon existing overhead levels
● the maximum affordable fixed overhead costs to break even on present sales volume and prices.

Time does not allow for precise financial analysis to be done. The need is for sufficiently accurate information to be produced quickly.

The newly appointed chief executive needs to avoid becoming consumed by fire fighting day-to-day problems. A dispassionate and detailed examination of the business must be the main priority. A good place to start is by spending some time with sales staff. Accompanying people on sales visits to clients and prospective clients is often revealing. The shortcomings of the company are likely to become transparent. Problems such as unsatisfactory product performance, uncompetitive prices, unacceptable quality and reliability, late delivery and ineffective selling will be exposed quickly.

Visits with sales staff will expose any shortcoming of the sales support team. So it makes sense to examine sales support departments next. Only then should attention be focused on marketing activities.

The contribution of marketing to the business needs to be measured. The level of expense needs to be assessed critically. It is all too easy for marketing activity to be confused with marketing effectiveness. In an actual case, the marketing staff was cut from 17 people to eight. Afterwards, it was generally accepted throughout the business that the contribution of marketing had increased substantially as a result of better direction, despite operating with a much smaller staff.

The production and delivery of the products or services supplied to customers should be the next point to come under scrutiny. Questions which need to be answered include:

- What scope is there to apply value-engineering techniques to the specification of products or services?
- What is the speed of delivery and the reliability of delivery promises?
- How much business is lost by late delivery or part delivery?
- What bottlenecks exist and how can these be overcome?
- What needs to be done to improve product or service quality and reliability?
- What can be done to reduce costs significantly?
- What make versus buy opportunities should be evaluated?
- What additional expenditure would produce an attractive financial return quickly?

The role and contribution of head office needs critical examination. The minimum possible number of staff needed should be determined. Wherever possible, operating businesses should be responsible for providing the full range of services needed in order to be managed as autonomous units.

Administration costs should be attacked. Satisfactory answers are needed to questions such as:

- What would happen if the work was left undone?
- Why is it done so often?
- Why is it done in such an expensive way?
- If it really needs to be done, how could it be handled at much lower cost?

Research and development can prove a difficult area to tackle. The chief executive appointed may lack technical knowledge compared to senior development staff. This need not necessarily be a disadvantage.

Questions to be answered which cut through the technical complexities include:

- How does the level of research and development expenditure compare with leading competitors?
- What percentage of total research and development costs are spent upon:
  - pure research?
  - new product development?
  - further development of existing products?
- What percentage of current sales is represented by new products or services introduced during the last five years?
- What is the percentage of sales from new products and services contributed by:
  - internal research and development?
  - licensing, royalty or distribution agreements?
  - joint venture co-operation?
- How are research and development projects evaluated commercially and financially before work is commenced?
- Is there adequate liaison between research and development, marketing and production staff?
- Are effective project-management and cost-control techniques used?
- Which projects have proved to be expensive failures, and what lessons have been learned?
- What new projects should be authorized or evaluated to meet the market needs?

Now we must address the need for rationalization of the business and a reduction in staff levels and overhead costs in order to achieve a break-even situation quickly. The range of products and services offered may need drastic pruning. A list of products and services in descending order of the amount of either marginal profit or gross profit produced by each one may be revealing. In an actual example, out of nearly 500 products six accounted for more than 80 per cent of the total marginal profit produced. Substantial reduction of the product range was achieved, without any significant adverse customer reaction.

Staff will have realized that redundancies will happen, without having been told. The sooner the redundancies are announced, the sooner the uncertainty is ended. In the meantime, the staff most likely to leave are the more talented people, who will find it easier to get other jobs – another reason for speed.

The overall number of people to be made redundant needs to be decided first, compatible with maintaining a viable infrastructure within the business and leaving an affordable level of overhead costs. Any suggestion of rateable cuts in each department must be rejected. The chief executive should agree with the manager of each department the number of redundancies required. Disproportionately large cuts may be required at head office and in administration departments. It is even possible that some modest recruitment may be necessary at the sharp end of the business, such as in direct sales staff or installation engineers.

Each manager should be required to propose a list showing the required redundancies. The chief executive should review each list, to be satisfied that an objective selection has been made. Then people need to be informed. This should be done face to face and handled with understanding, generosity and compassion. Trade unions will need to be notified where appropriate. If possible, help should be given to assist people to obtain other jobs. There is no ideal time to announce redundancies, but a Friday afternoon makes sense. This means that only those people still employed with the company will return to work on the following Monday morning. Disaffected people who have been made redundant must not be allowed to linger on.

It is important that all of the redundancies should be announced at one time. Morale will be affected, but much worse so if people are left to speculate when the next round of redundancies will be announced. The sooner that the business needs to start recruiting people again, the better it is for morale.

At this stage, the reduced level of fixed costs will be known by the chief executive and the overall percentage marginal profit presently achieved. So it is easy to calculate the annual sales value required to break even. This should be translated into a monthly sales target needed to break even, and the management team should collectively be committed to the goal of the first month in which the break-even sales value will be exceeded and so eliminate the losses.

The next step should be to involve the board or executive committee in setting revised and demanding sales and profit forecasts for the remainder of the current year. The opportunity should be taken to improve monthly management information in order to provide people with the information needed to manage the business effectively.

Rigorous budget preparation is needed for the next financial year. People must realize that the elimination of losses is not enough; it is only the first and relatively easy stage on the road to financial recovery. The goal must be to achieve an acceptable return on the operating assets employed as quickly as possible.

In a turn-round situation, an important part of the budget should be a number of profit-improvement projects, with each one:

- designed to achieve rapid profit improvement
- having a member of the board accountable for timely and successful completion.

Once the initial surgery has been carried out and profit-improvement projects initiated, it is time to get down to business development in earnest. A fundamental issue needs to be addressed. Now that initial turn-round work has been done, should the chief executive continue? Or be replaced by someone better suited to carry out the business-development work? This may seem a surprising question to raise. It may well be, however, that the turn-round person is not ideally suited to stay on through the medium term to achieve the business development needed.

The evidence available shows that surgery and short-term profit-improvement action are likely to eliminate losses but that major new initiatives are needed to achieve an acceptable financial return.

There is no substitute for:

- creating a vision statement
- adopting the quantum leap approach
- identifying and evaluating strategic options
- establishing an effective organization structure
- setting up major business-development projects.

Business Plans

In this chapter we are not talking about putting forward ideas, proposals, etc. for approval, but about preparing a formal, written business plan. This chapter and Chapter 10 are complementary.

11.1   Introduction

Preparing and presenting business plans takes up a large chunk of any manager's business life. Whether seeking internal approval (e.g. from the board) or external finance (e.g. from a bank or venture capitalist), the business plan is a crucial document. The focus of the plan should be on:

- setting realistic goals for activities and performance
- demonstrating how objectives will be met
- identifying the resources required to achieve the plan.

Any business plan should also provide a yardstick against which the actual outcome can be measured.

All business plans need regular appraisal and updating.

11.2   Key ingredients

Depending on its precise use, a plan should be tailored accordingly. Indeed, while certain information can be common, various manifestations of the same essential plan can vary in shape and size to suit a range of precise functions.

This section provides a framework which can be used for any permutation. Not all points will be relevant or they may need to be slightly adapted to suit particular circumstances.

A typical contents page (and there should always be one) of a business plan would include:

(1) executive summary
(2) background
(3) main products and/or services
(4) market analysis and marketing
(5) manufacturing and operations
(6) management
(7) organization and personnel
(8) ownership
(9) financial analysis
(10) risks and rewards
(11) objectives and milestones
(12) appendices

The length of a business plan is determined by its purpose and the target audience. Great care should always be taken with the executive summary (no more than one page is desirable) and the plan proper should be as short as precise communication and the subject matter can allow with any back-up information being relegated to appendices.

1. Executive summary

This should cover concisely:

- the purpose of the plan
- description of the business and its markets
- summary of success factors
- funding required
- three to five years financial projections (turnover and net profit).

2. Background

This should be a short 'history' pointing up the success elements and relating the past (primarily successes) to future objectives, particularly indicating where objectives set in the past have since been met.

3. Main products and/or services

This should describe the main products and/or services, their competitive advantage in the market-place and how future developments will yield even greater success. Any technological intellectual property, regulatory and R&D advantages should be defined.

Depending on the nature of the products/services it may be useful to go into detail on such aspects as the development cycle of new products/services; what new products/services are planned to follow-on from those offered at the start; how protected (from a patent, trade mark or copyright position) is each product/service.

4. Market analysis and marketing

This part is absolutely crucial and in order to present a convincing business plan (and more importantly in order to be able to meet the planned objectives) it will need to present facts about the market-place (including the competition) and precise details of how the marketing activities planned will give the market share predicted. So, how should this part of the plan be tackled? It is recommended that you break it down into four parts.

(1) The industry/sector
The industry/sector that you are in needs to be defined in terms of:

- its main characteristics,
- its main customers
- the applications for your products/ services,
- the likely trends and
- the outlook (changes in size, etc.) over the next five years.

(2) The market
Segments targeted

- What are major areas aimed at?
- Where are they?
- How are they changing/developing?

Customer success factors in each segment targeted

- What are the critical elements (re-liability, quality, price, service, etc.)?
- What is the customer profile (size of company, identity of decision maker, number of customers)?
- What are the buying habits (size of orders, competitive tendering, supplier approval, changeability) seasonal variations?
- What success already achieved with customers or what interest shown to date?

(3) The competition
Due weight must be given to an appraisal of current and likely future competitors, with theirs and your strengths and weaknesses objectively assessed.

- Who are the competitors, now (and

likely in the future)?
- How do you compare?
- How will they respond?
- Why will you succeed?

(4) The marketing activities

These need to be separated into marketing and sales

- Marketing
  Your plans for positioning the products/ services in terms of quality, price, service, etc. should be set out, and details given of plans for:
  - distribution
  - promotion and advertising
  - pricing (demand or cost based, discounts, planned levels for the future?)
  - customer service and support
  - geographical penetration (domestic, international)
  - prioritizing opportunities.
- Sales
  You will need to show how sales will be achieved (through retail outlets, agents, franchises, a sales force?) and how prospective customers will be identified and converted into actual customers. The plan for operating through agents, etc. will need to be set out showing terms, conditions and predictions. For operating a sales force, the detail should include size and geographical coverage, productivity (calls and conversion rates, average size of each sale, repeat order pattern) and remuneration systems (basic and commission levels).
  For retail outlets, site size, sales staff, sales per square foot, etc. will need to be cited with back-up evidence.

5. Manufacturing and operations

This section needs to home in on how production will be accomplished or how service operations will be carried out identifying:

- the production service/service process
- suppliers (sources both internal and external) and what are the likely developments
- key production/operating advantages
- present facilities, capacity and future plans
- critical aspects (parts, machinery, etc.)
- costs of production (and impact of volume on them).

6. Management

Details should be provided in summary form of the following:

- the Board of directors (indicating experience and expertise)
- key managers (again indicating experience and expertise)
- how key people will be retained (salaries/bonuses/incentives, etc.)
- recruitment plans.

7. Organization and personnel

A summary of staff members, functions and organization charts should be given and plans for recruitment, retention and remuneration outlined.

8. Ownership

Details of the degree of control held by directors and managers and staff should be given with a summary of other main shareholdings.

9. Financial analysis

It is vital that financial information is presented in an accessible way in this section of the plan, bearing in mind that full financial projections will be provided in the appendices, and concentration should be on:

- summarizing key data
  Sales and profit before tax for three to five years ahead (and back if available)
- commenting on key aspects (particularly assumptions used) of the projections for:
  - sales
  - direct costs
  - overheads
  - cash flow
- identifying the most realistic outcome
- showing funds required and when
- how investors/owners could exit (e.g. listing, sale, etc.).

10. Risks and rewards

- The risks should be identified and the ways in which they can be dealt with need to be summarized.
- The possible value of the company if the plan is met should be set out (and that valuation backed up by market-place evidence).

11. Objectives and milestones

It is important to define the objectives (of each main business unit) and to provide a timetable for each relevant component of the plan (product/service, marketing, manufacturing, management, etc.).

12. Appendices

Likely contents of the appendices will include:

- financial history – latest audited accounts
- financial projections for three to five years
  - balance sheets
  - capital expenditure forecasts
  - cash-flow forecasts
  - details of assumptions behind the figures
  - sensitivity analysis for key factors (e.g. if a milestone were missed what would be the impact)
- marketing plan
- full details of products/services
- CVs of key managers
- details of key tangible assets (e.g. property) and intangible assets (e.g. patents, trademarks, copyrights, etc.)
- organizational charts
- technical terms, etc. explained.

Acquisitions and Disposals of Unquoted Companies

This section deals with the acquisitions and disposals of unquoted companies and not with the takeover of a 'public' company. It is written in summary, check-list style to point up the key areas for attention to indicate possible pitfalls. The structure of the section is as follows:

- buying
- selling
- negotiating
- managing post-completion.

As in every deal there will be a buyer and a seller the whole section is relevant to each player in the acquisition/disposal process. NB The check-list approach taken precludes examination of detailed aspects, including the tax and legal issues.

In *Business Week* (15 January 1990) an analysis of various acquisition deals (which had worked and which had not) concluded that the keys to a good deal are:

- have a strategic purpose
- know the business
- investigate thoroughly
- make realistic assumptions
- don't pay too much
- don't borrow too much
- integrate carefully and fast.

12.1 Buying

1. How to plan for succession acquisitions

(1) Select attractive market segments and countries

- based on assessment of:
  - future market demand and capacity
  - existing and likely competitors
  - ease of entry by acquisition or start-up.
- wherever attractive, pursue opportunities for:
  - market leadership
  - increased market share.

(2) Define commercial rationale for acquiring the target

- analyse sound reasons (as well as selecting market segments) e.g.
  - extending product range
  - acquiring key sales outlets
  - protecting a source of supply
  - the minimum profits required
  - the shape of the organization into which it will fit
  - the desired location(s)
  - the key features for success.

2. How to find attractive sellers

(1) Use the knowledge within the business

- brainstorm
- brief buyers, salespeople, technical staff
- identify what else your customers buy
- visit your sales outlets and see what else they sell.

(2) Desk research prospective targets

- in the UK this could include reviewing these sources:
  - Jordans/ICC Market Sector surveys
  - Top 10,000 Unquoted Companies
  - Key British Enterprises
  - Kompass Regional Guides
  - Electronic Databases
  - trade associations, press and exhibitions.

(3) Put bread on the water

- include a paragraph in annual report
- get editorial coverage in trade press
- make use of specialist newsletters on acquisitions and disposals
- when press releasing an acquisition – say 'more wanted'.

(4) Involve intermediaries and advisers

- notify intermediaries and professional advisers
  - major accountants – disposal register (cost about 1.5 per cent)
  - business brokers (cost on scale: 5 to 1 per cent)
  - merchant banks and specialist advisers (cost about 2 per cent, including professional advice)
  - venture capital funds seeking a sale.
- consider outside help for acquisition search
  - agree acquisition profile
  - demand exclusivity.
- beware of buying what is for sale instead of what you want to buy.

3. Consider alternatives to acquisition

(1) Start-up

- internal resources needed
- external funding needed
- viability of a start-up plan in practical, time and cost terms.

(2) Distribution or manufacturing rights

- as a way of getting to know target
- as an alternative to acquisition.

(3) Minority equity stake

- to lead to eventual acquisition with a formula for control or purchase
- to obtain a non-executive directorship for influence.

(4) Joint venture or consortium

- pick compatible partners
- anticipate corporate culture problems
- establish management accountability
- identify exit routes.

(5) Majority equity control

- may be useful overseas.

(6) Earn out deals

- relevant for many private companies
- beware of pitfalls (see later).

4. Agree an acquisition profile

(1) Write it down

- to focus the search
- to pre-sell internally
- to avoid abortive effort
- to brief intermediaries.

(2) Write an acquisition profile giving

- the nature of the business, the products/services required
- the maximum price affordable
- the nature of the consideration (e.g. cash, shares, loan stock, etc.)

(3) Consider using outside help

- short-list targets (accounts and product/service literature)
- list rejected companies (and state key reason)
- adviser to telephone key person to explore sale
- agree completion date and fee
- legal completion fee (about 1.5 per cent)
- don't pay retainers.

(4) Advertise selectively and effectively

- The *Financial Times* and *Wall Street Journal*, e.g. reaches owners and intermediaries
- tradepress – less expensive
- avoid box number – puts people off
- specify market sector, profit and location – give company name, person and telephone number.

5. How to handle the initial approach

- telephone preferred to writing
- private company (find out key shareholder or institutional investors)
- subsidiary (approach the group)
- use an approach by a third party
  - to protect identity initially
  - to 'sell' a possibly unwelcome acquirer

- to save management time
- to benefit from their expertise.

6. How to approach the investigation needed before negotiation proceeds

- to confirm your wish to buy
- to identify skeletons and hidden gold, e.g.
  - tax irregularities
  - recent loss of major customers
  - overseas opportunities unexploited
  - cost rationalization opportunities
  - surplus assets and working capital
- to project future profits and cash flows
- to focus due diligence investigation if deal agreed.

7. How to carry out a comprehensive assessment of the target. Check out:

- sales history and projections (and identify one-offs)
- key customers, suppliers, contracts
- pricing (opportunity to increase or need to hold?)
- order book (is it an 'asset' or 'liability'?)
- distribution channels
- competitors
- production capacity and efficiency
- cost of refurbishment
- capital investment needed for expansion
- accounting policies and provisions
- R&D projects
- key people
- salaries, bonuses, fringe benefits
- share option schemes
- pension fund
  - contracted in or out?
  - over or under funded?
  - insured or invested?

- money purchase or final salary?
● health and safety issues
● contingent liabilities, e.g.
  - litigation threat
  - warranty claims
  - environmental pollution time bomb
● compatibility of corporate culture and style
● owner extravagances
  - spouses and/or relatives employed
  - planes, boats, houses
  - entertainment and sponsorship.

8. How to use investigating accountants effectively

● meet the team leader
● agree written terms of reference
● insist on a budgetary fee limit
● agree number of people and timetable
● start only after heads of agreement signed
● set date for receipt of report
● ask for verbal debrief as well
(● it is not essential to use your auditing firm).

9. How to handle overseas acquisitions

(1) Select the country

● political stability
  - civil unrest
  - national strikes
  - local wars.
● cultural and social background
  - discrimination against foreign ownership?
  - language skills

- education standards
- employee relations
- communications and services
- acceptance of expatriates
- expatriates' safety.
● legal requirements
  - equity ownership restrictions
  - government agency approval needed
  - monopoly and anti-trust considerations
  - exchange control
  - employment law
  - reporting requirements.
● taxation and repatriation of funds
  - taxation rate
  - incentives and tariffs
  - withholding taxes
  - double taxation agreements
  - repatriation of profits and capital.

(2) Within the chosen country

● stick to market segments/business you know
● check sufficient acquisition candidates exist
● likely purchase price
● merit of local equity partner as a minority investor
● learn from their banks in the UK
● choice of advisors?
  - overseas bank (contact UK branch first)
  - management consultants
  - auditors (overseas branches)
  - local lawyers
● acquisition search
  - known targets
  - search based in the country.

12.2   Selling

1. How to plan a successful sale

(1) Consider the alternatives to selling

- management buy-out or buy-in
- sell equity stake to financial institution
- merge, using 'paper' (i.e. shares not cash)
- acquire (with institutional backing)
- buy-in some of own shares
- obtain a stock-market listing
  - reported profit before tax needed:
    Unlisted Securities Market: £0.5m+
    Full listing: £1m+

(2) Decide when to sell

- show current year progress and future growth
- avoid a recent set-back or a loss
- people often hold on too long
- beware of serious illness
- realize temporary scarcity value
- approaching year end is a good time.

(3) Decide what to sell

- related businesses, e.g.
  - overseas subsidiaries
  - another business which conflicts
- shares or assets and business
- property to be included or excluded.

(4) Preparation needed to get the best price

- ensure share structure simple

- avoid shares held by children under 18
- corporation tax, VAT and PAYE (in order and up to date?)
- capital gains tax planning
- budgets, monthly accounts and year-end forecasts give confidence
- assess freehold and leasehold value
- employment contracts in order
- pension fund (especially transfer from a group)
- intellectual property (transfer ownership or give licence)
- acceptable staff incentive schemes
- no major litigation in progress or pending
- share option scheme implications.

2. How to find attractive buyers

(1) use the knowledge within the business

- always record unsolicited approaches
- identify companies:
  - offering related products/services
  - with a product/service gap
  - with a similar business in other countries
- direct competitors may be less attractive purchasers.

(2) involve a professional adviser

- business brokers
  - no deal/no fee basis
  - unlikely to provide professional advice
  - beware of gossip factor.
- major accounting firms
  - challenge joining disposal register
  - will provide professional advice on a fee basis.
- specialist adviser

– will provide professional advice
– may specialize in smaller deals
– minimum fee say £25,000 for completed deal.

(3) Consider advertising

● may produce unexpected purchasers
● don't reveal identity unintentionally
● FT reaches buyers and intermediaries
● ask for written responses
● may produce 40 to 125 replies (buyers, advisers, individuals)
● eliminate unwanted replies
● get confidentiality agreement signed
● then send written synopsis.

(4) Use a controlled auction, if appropriate

● consider controlled auction
    – when firmly committed to sell
    – confident acceptable offer obtainable
    – prepare detailed sales memorandum
    – announce by press release or advert
    – and/or approach target buyers
● handle a controlled auction
    – get confidentiality agreement signed
    – send out sales memorandum
    – set date for outline offers
    – short-list buyers to meet management

– seller may give standard contract
– invite confirmed/revised offers
– negotiate with preferred purchaser.

3. How to handle approaches

(1) From an intermediary

● check them out
● find out company and individual represented.

(2) From a prospective purchaser

● if interested, meet on neutral ground
● establish authority of individual
● may provide market knowledge or business opportunity
● be guarded
● take professional advice at outset
● consider seeking other purchasers

(3) Agree, before any on-site investigation

● ball park price or valuation basis
● scale of on-site investigation
    – probably two or three people
    – for about a day.
● information not to be provided until heads of agreement signed, e.g.
    – customer analysis
    – research know-how.

12.3 Negotiating

1. How to value the business

(1) Buyers

● should base their valuation on:
  - their projections of profits and cash flows
  - any upstream or downstream benefits.
● should assess
  - balance sheet worth and surplus assets
  - cost/time of alternatives to acquisitions.

(2) Sellers

● should assess
  - value from the buyer's standpoint
  - other buyer or options
  - effect on their life style and retirement
  - if a sale now is premature
  - strategic significance or rarity value.

(3) Calculation of adjusted profits for most recent year

● buyers should adjust profit before tax for changes that will be made, e.g.
  - different accounting policies, depreciation
  - need to appoint finance director
  - higher insurance cover needed
  - wage and salary differentials
  - additional pension costs.
● Sellers will point out:

  - excessive directors' salaries and pensions
  - cost of relatives no longer employed
  - boats and planes
  - allocated management changes
  - significant one-off event, e.g. a large bad debt or revenue costs of US launch relocation costs.

(4) Calculation of adjusted profits and cash flows for current and future years should identify

● assumptions used in forecasts
● what the buyer can add, e.g.
  - additional sales opportunities
  - cost rationalization and reduction
  - tighter financial control
  - upstream or downstream benefits.

2. How to assess the value of the business

(1) Price earnings ratio (widely used, but ignores cash flow)

● attempts to calculate 'market value'
● provides useful benchmark for sellers
● PE ratio = $\dfrac{\text{Current share price}}{\text{Earnings per share}}$
● empirical evidence shows unquoted companies often sell at a discount to listed PEs.
  - discount may be at least 20 per cent and up to 50 per cent unless strategic significance or rarity value exists (when a premium PE ratio may be obtained).

(2) Return on investment (gives short-/medium-term indicator)

- ROI = $\dfrac{\text{Profit before tax}}{\text{Net investment}}$
- Net investment = Purchase price plus further cash investment needed, minus surplus assets realized
- many listed companies making acquisitions seek at least 25 per cent ROI in second full financial year after acquisition.

(3) Discounted cash flow (Chapter 6 addresses key issues of cash flow) in acquisitions deals
Initial investment = Initial purchase price
Annual cash flow = Cash generated/ needed for operations plus surplus assets realized minus earn-out payments

- use percentage of internal rate of return and discounted pay-back period
- use sensitivity analysis of 'what if?' questions.

(4) Net asset backing (relevant for loss makers)

- seek to buy at a discount to net assets because:
  - relieving owners of a problem may need a safety margin.

(5) Take into account

- impact on earnings per share (important for listed companies)
  - calculate impact of current year's earnings per share
  - check when any dilution eliminates
  - take into account earn-out payments
- rarity or scarcity value (premium others may be prepared to pay).

(6) Worked example of valuation (for non-accountants)

	£'000
Previous year profit before tax of seller	325
effect of buyer's depreciation policy	20
Allow for extra cost of:	
Financial Director	(45)
Wage and salary differentials	(25)
Higher insurance cover	(10)
Add back:	
Excess cost of directors' salaries and personal pensions	120
Relatives no longer required	45
Annual cost of company boat	30
Adjusted profit before tax	460

	Last year	This year	Next year	Year after
Adjusted profit before tax	460	530	570	620
the buyer will add	—	10	50	80
Incremental profit before tax	460	540	620	700
assume 35 per cent corporation tax	(160)	(190)	(220)	(245)
Incremental profit after tax	300	350	400	455

Assume the sector average PE ratio =	12.5
Assume a discount of 20 per cent =	(2.5)
Earnings multiple to be paid	10.0

Likely purchase price $= 10.0 \times \pounds300,000 = \pounds3m$

If buyer wanted 25 per cent ROI in year after next:

Likely purchase price $= \pounds700,000$ divided by 25 per cent

$= \pounds2.8m$

(Assuming no further investment or cash surplus)

3. How to approach an earn-out deal

(1) Basis of an earn-out deal

- buy 100 per cent of equity now
- pay some purchase consideration initially, to reflect
  - reasonable price for profits to date
  - not less than net asset backing
- additional payments or increased future profits before tax
- sellers should think carefully about earn out periods longer than the next two years
- buyers should put a cap or maximum limit on earn-out payments.

(2) An earn-out deal makes sense if:

- business success still depends on owners
- asset backing low (e.g. service company)
- profits forecast to increase rapidly
- profits at risk (e.g. loss of a major customer)
- an owner is to continue as MD.

(3) Earn-out issues to be addressed by the seller include:

- definition of profit before tax for earn-out and contract needs to specify:
  - accounting policies
  - management charges (e.g. payroll and legal, etc.)
  - costs of central services used (e.g. distribution)
  - intra-group pricing policies
  - cost of finance to be provided
  - dividend policy.
- capital gains tax implications
  - if all the earn-out payments are paper (i.e. shares or debentures or loan notes) then capital gains tax liability is rolled over
  - expert advice is needed before negotiating.
- management' control:
  - need to agree before structuring deal:
    changes which will alter costs (e.g. appointment of financial director)
    business opportunities to be pursued (e.g. start up in USA next year)
    no-go areas (e.g. competing against other subsidiaries)
  - need to establish at the outset:
    board control
    preparation of budgets, monthly accounts and year end forecasts, sensitive issues (e.g. initiating litigation or dealing with the media)
  (NB: to buyers – if business starts to fall apart – move in!).

(4) Worked example of earn-out deal (for non-accountants):

- Consider a company providing computer training courses. Growth depends upon three owners recruiting and training more trainees, as well as aggressive marketing. The net asset backing is only $325,000.

Another $400,000 cash will be needed for expansion by the year after next.

	Last year	This year	Next year	Year after
Adjusted profit before tax	225	400	600	850
Assume 35 per cent corporation tax	(80)	(140)	(210)	(300)
Adjusted profit after tax	145	260	390	550

The deal agreed was:

$1.2 million initially
plus $0.2 million for achieving $400,000 this year
plus twice profits in excess of $400,000 next year
and the year after, up to a maximum of $1.3m

$$\text{Initial PE ratio} = \frac{\$1.2m}{\$145,000} = 8.3$$

$$\text{Final PE ratio} = \frac{\$2.7m}{\$550,000} = 4.9$$

$$\text{ROI year after next} = \frac{\$850,000}{\$2.7m + \$0.4m} = 27 \text{ per cent}$$

4. How to negotiate the deal

(1) Skills required

- previous experience
- negotiation expertise
- tax and legal knowledge.

(2) Helpful elements

- keep team as small as possible
- set a negotiation price limit at outset
- identify any deal-breaker issues.

(3) Deal format stage of negotiation, discuss and agree:

- share purchase versus assets and business
- outright purchase versus earn-out deal
- assets to be excluded
- directors and relatives to retire/resign
- attractive forms of purchase consideration
- conditional purchase contract (to defer capital gains tax a year)
- date for final negotiation.

(4) Possible forms of purchase consideration

- cash
- shares

- loanstock or loan notes
- pre-completion dividend
- personal pension contributions
- purchase of assets
- service contracts
- consultancy agreements.

(5) Typical agenda for final negotiation

- update since last meeting
- confirmation of what is included
- purchase by directors of assets (e.g. cars/boats)
- contracts for directors/key staff
- treatment of existing share options
- transfer of pension fund
- intellectual property
- earn-out formula and period
- key warranties and indemnities

- purchase price and consideration
- timetable to legal completion.

(6) Timetable to legal completion

- Signing of heads of agreements or letter of intent including:
  - period of exclusivity
  - non-disclosure
  - any cost indemnity for vendors
- receipt of share purchase agreement
- start and duration of accounting investigation
- receipt by buyer of accountants report
- date reserved for principals and lawyers to finalize contract
- receipt of disclosure statement
- place and venue of signing contract.

12.4 Managing post-completion

1. Prepare for first day

- first impressions count
- listen to advice from vendors
- involve continuing directors in announcement
- plan to tell customers and suppliers
- notify trade unions as appropriate
- prepare and plan for day one.

2. Handle first day successfully

- meet management, staff and unions
- consider a meeting for announcements, e.g. with corporate videos and questions

- prepare for anticipated questions
- avoid rash assurances
- demonstrate a real interest and concern
- recognize rumours and anxiety abound
- tell your own staff who may be affected.

3. Achieve financial control immediately (concentrate on essentials)

- capital investment and special revenue expense authorization
- cash management
- head count and expense control
- reliable sales and profit forecasting.

4. Introduce uniform budgeting and reporting carefully

- immediate reporting changes may cause accounting chaos

- key requirement is reliable profit and cash figures for rest of year
- introduce uniform budgeting and reporting for new financial year
- need to train accountants and sell benefits to managers.

5. Manage and integrate the business effectively

- consider non-executive chairman to
  - lead board meetings
  - help pursue opportunities with rest of group
  - restrict unnecessary visits by group staff
- identify special skills of owners

  - have a plan to eliminate vulnerability (e.g. major customer contract, technical expertise, etc.) and make sure it is complete before end of year of earn-out
- recognize dangers of forcing culture change on successful company
- assess the existing management talent
- consider injecting an MD designate, with a 'real' job
- arrange staff exchanges and visits
- visit major consumers, suppliers and overseas operations at board levels
- learn from the acquisition
- for a loss-maker, appoint a full-time MD immediately.